Kingdom Capital: A Christian Guide to Investing Real Estate

Author: Andrew Driver

Publisher: Self

Publication Year: 2023

To you the reader,

I pray that this journey through the pages of this book may inspire you to navigate the intricate waters of real estate investing, not solely as a financial endeavor, but as an opportunity to serve God and His kingdom. As you read and reflect on the biblical wisdom shared within these pages, may it deepen your faith, elevate your understanding, and equip you to align your investment strategies with God's perfect will. In God's Grace, Amen.

Sincerely,

Andrew Driver

Table of Contents

Introduction

Introduction

The Influence of Real Estate Investing on One's Ability to Achieve Financial Independence, Faith, and Fortitude
We want to take this opportunity to welcome you, dear reader, to the journey of real estate investing, a trip where faith meets

action, a journey packed with chances, and a journey blessed by the grace of God. Despite the fact that it is fraught with difficulties, this way of life affords a variety of benefits that are in harmony with the teachings of Proverbs 13:22, which states, "A good person leaves an inheritance for their children's children." These benefits include financial independence, the creation of wealth, and a sense of accomplishment that is in line with the Christian principles of faithfulness, stewardship, and expansion.

The fact that real estate may generate profits in a variety of different ways makes it a desirable choice as an investment vehicle. When you make an investment in real estate, you are not only securing gains from asset appreciation; you are also producing a stream of income through rents, and you are leveraging the tax benefits; all of this is done while obeying the Biblical ideal of wise stewardship (Luke 14:28).

Realization and Command of the Situation

The verse found in Proverbs 24:3-4 informs us that "by wisdom a house is built, and by understanding it is established; by knowledge the rooms are filled with all precious and pleasant riches." Real estate, which is a practical and tangible asset, exemplifies this scripture to the fullest. You have the ability to see, touch, and develop your properties, which provides a sense of security and control that is unmatched by stocks or bonds. Your knowledge and common sense when it comes to the upkeep and improvement of your property have a direct impact on both its value and the return on investment you receive.

Security and Resistance to Harm

Real estate, much like precious treasure and oil,' provides a robust and secure kind of investment. The wisdom of Proverbs 21:20 underlines the prudence of storing up valuable assets: "Precious treasure and oil are in a wise man's dwelling, but a foolish man devours it." Even while real estate markets have swings from time to time, property values have a history of rising steadily over the long run, making them a good hedge against inflation. In addition, rental properties have the potential to produce a consistent flow of revenue, much like the widow's jar in the narrative of Elisha in 2 Kings 4:1-7, which continued to receive a continual supply of oil.

The Accumulation of Wealth

Many of the most successful people in the world have used real estate as a means to build and multiply their wealth, serving as a living example of the parable of the talents (Matthew 25:14–30). The wealth-creation potential of real estate is well-documented, and it resonates with Deuteronomy 8:18, which reminds us that it is God "who gives you the ability to produce wealth."

The Effective Use of Leverage

Leverage is a concept that is consistent with the biblical doctrine of sowing and reaping, which is found in 2 Corinthians 9:6. Leverage can be utilized while investing in real estate. You can acquire control of a sizeable property with only a modest amount of your own money and by borrowing the remainder of the funds necessary. As time passes and the value of the property increases, it is possible that your return on investment will be based on the total worth of the property; this exemplifies the sowing-reaping principle in action.

Investing in real estate can, in addition to the financial gains it provides, bring about a great deal of personal fulfillment and spiritual development. It is possible to find fulfillment in a task by emulating the transformative work that God does in our life (Philippians 1:6) through the renovation of an old, run-down property into a lovely home. Investing in real estate can also contribute to personal growth, which can improve your decision-making abilities in a variety of aspects of life. This is due to the knowledge and experience that is gained through the endeavor.

Dave Ramsey, a well-known Christian financial guru, frequently quotes the following passage from the book of Proverbs: "The diligent make use of all they find (Proverbs 12:27)," which refers to the possibilities of real estate investments when handled with a diligent and faithful frame of mind.

Your journey as an investor in real estate should be approached with the mindset that it is a journey of faith, one that requires learning, growth, and the application of Christian principles. Remember, as you navigate this wonderful field, that the keys to unlocking the full rewards of real estate ownership are patience, effort, deliberate planning, and most significantly, dependence on God's wisdom. This is the best advice I can give you as you navigate this interesting sector.

Why Choose This Book?

You might be wondering why you would need this book in a world that is rife with investment manuals, real estate instruction books, and words of financial wisdom. Why should you spend your precious time, effort, and resources reading these pages? This book presents a one-of-a-kind combination of practical advice, biblical principles, and the tried-and-true wisdom of Christian investors. That combination is where the answer can be found.

According to Matthew 6:21, "For where your treasure is, there your heart will be also." This book was written from the heart, with the earnest purpose of guiding you towards a successful path that is in alignment with your beliefs and values. Investing in real estate is not only a method for accumulating wealth; it is also a way to steward God's benefits in a way that is both responsible and successful.

The advice that is crammed into these pages is meant to serve as your compass as you navigate the exciting world of real estate. We go deeply into the foundations, explore advanced tactics, and take you through the exciting twists and turns that are a part of the real estate environment. The purpose of this guide is to provide you with information that has been gleaned from the experiences of prominent Christian real estate professionals and prosperous investors who have navigated these waters guided by their faith.

However, the purpose of this book is not only to give knowledge. It is intended to motivate people to take action. In the same way that the Apostle Paul exhorted the readers of Hebrews 10:24, "And let us consider how we may spur one another on toward love and good deeds," the purpose of this book is to ignite your drive to produce substantial riches while sticking to the principles of the Bible.

This book contains biblical stories, examples from real life, and activities that are meant to put those lessons into practice. The goals of the book are to encourage interaction, critical analysis, and personal development. Each chapter stands on its own as a pillar of information, but when taken as a whole, this book provides you with a detailed road map to help you navigate the world of real estate investment.

In addition to that, it serves as a toolkit for one's own personal development. It takes into account not only knowledge of finances but also the cultivation of a positive mindset that is faith-centered as well as resilience, both of which are essential for flourishing in the real estate sector. The Bible advises us in Proverbs 4:23, "Above all else, guard your heart, for everything you do flows from it."

Consider this book to be your guide as you navigate the waters of reconciling your desire for financial success with your Christian beliefs. It is more than a book; it is a compass that will direct you through the treacherous terrain of the real estate market while allowing you to remain true to your Christian beliefs. Thank you for joining us. Together, let's get started on this path that leads to development, success, and faith.

Instructions for Using This Book

This book is your all-inclusive guide to real estate investing since it contains a mix of practical counsel, scriptural direction, and Christian ideals. The fact that it may be applied to your specific journey toward being a good steward of God's blessings is what gives it its value; its potential to convey wisdom is only one aspect of that value.

According to Matthew 7:8, "For everyone who asks receives; the one who seeks finds; and to the one who knocks, the door will be opened." Reading this book from beginning to end is the best way to get the most out of what it has to offer, so we strongly recommend doing so. The chapters are organized in a logical succession, with each one building upon the knowledge gained in the prior chapter to provide a comprehensive comprehension of real estate investment. Your understanding of the interconnection of the many facets of real estate investing will be enhanced as you proceed through this step-by-step guide, which provides a comprehensive picture.

The beauty of this book, on the other hand, is that its usefulness is not limited to only the first reading. Each chapter can be read independently, and each one provides insightful information about a different facet of real estate investment. Think of them as checkpoints or reference points along the way. These chapters are your go-to resource whether you are making your first property acquisition, adopting a different investing plan, or navigating through a challenge. They can help you in any of these situations.

The topics that are presented are brought to life through the use of real-world examples, actionable advice, and insightful statements from well-known Christian investors scattered throughout this book. Spend some time thinking about these pearls of wisdom; they provide peeks into how theory and practice come together in the world of real estate.

It is said in Proverbs 24:3-4 that "by wisdom a house is built, and through understanding it is established; through knowledge its rooms are filled with rare and beautiful treasures." Learning isn't only about taking in information; it's also about reflecting on that information, comprehending it, and putting it into practice. This is an interactive book that will help you apply what you learn to your specific situation by providing you with activities, questions for self-reflection, and other prompts throughout the text.

Keep in mind that this book is not merely a resource; rather, it is a tool that is both dynamic and interactive. Engage with it, think deeply about the lessons it teaches, put its ideas into practice in real-world situations, and return to its pages as you make forward on your path. The real value of this book is not found in simply reading it; rather, it is found in utilizing it as a guidepost for your trip through the world of real estate. This book will assist you in investing your resources in a manner that is sensible and that brings respect to God.

The Importance of Maintaining a Faith-Based Mental Attitude When Investing in Real Estate

Many people have the misconception that investing in real estate is primarily a financial venture, a game of numbers, and a focus on profit margins. Your mental condition, in particular when examined through the lens of Christian religion and beliefs, plays a huge influence, and although financial savvy is essential, there is another factor that plays a significant role that is frequently disregarded.

Every step along the way, our mental state, which is formed by our beliefs, emotions, attitudes, and mindset, has an effect on how much money we make and how much we lose. It dictates how we deal with uncertainty, how we respond to obstacles, how we commit to our goals, and how we adjust to different situations. As our mental state becomes more aligned with Christian principles, we find that we are guided not by monetary rewards but rather by a feeling of purpose and stewardship in everything we do.

Patience, as a virtue, is described here. The process of investing in real estate is more of a marathon than a sprint. Because it is a commitment over a prolonged period of time, it takes time and patience before yielding meaningful rewards. As the verse from Galatians 6:9 tells us, "Let us not become weary in doing good, for at the proper time we will reap a harvest if we do not give up." Patience is essential in waiting for the right investment, allowing your property to appreciate, and persevering through slower market cycles.

Have the Courage to Confront Risks Every investment comes with some level of risk, whether it is swings in the market, unexpected costs, or vacancy periods. A faith-driven mindset enables you to confront risks with courage and confidence, making calculated decisions that are backed by diligent research. Joshua 1:9 says, "Have I not commanded you? Be strong and courageous. Do not be afraid; do not be discouraged, for the LORD your God will be with you wherever you go."

Resistance to Defeat when It Occurs. There will be occasions in which investments will not go according to plan. These issues, such as unforeseen maintenance, downturns in the market, and difficulties in selling a property, can be disappointing. Nevertheless, the Bible tells us in Romans 5:3-4 that "we also glory in our sufferings," because we know that suffering generates perseverance, and perseverance produces character, and character produces hope.

The world of real estate investment is a complex and ever-changing one, and humility keeps us open to learning and always refining our tactics. The Bible states in Proverbs 1:5, "Let the wise listen and add to their learning, and let the discerning get guidance."

Love and emotional intelligence go hand in hand. Interacting with a wide variety of people is required in the real estate industry, including fellow investors, tenants, brokers, and contractors. Your capacity to control your emotions and comprehend people, which is a sort of love, has a significant impact on how successful you will be. In the book of 1 Peter chapter 4, verse 8, it is written, "Above all, love each other deeply, because love covers over a multitude of sins." Throughout the entirety of this book, we will go further into each of these mental state components, studying techniques to cultivate these qualities and learning how they may help you become a successful real estate investor who is also a steward of God's provisions. Let's begin.

Laying the Foundation

Gaining an Understanding of Real Estate from a Biblical Standpoint

We would like to take this opportunity to welcome you to the exciting world of real estate investment, a world that is teeming with opportunities, growth, and promise. When you set out on this road, you will experience the exhilaration of achieving financial freedom, the enticement of accumulating riches, and the profound joy of making a difference in people's lives, all of which are bolstered by the teachings of Christ. Investing in real estate is unique. It goes beyond standard buy-and-hold methods and provides a variety of other opportunities for profit. The principle of multiplication is shown in the Parable of the Talents found in Matthew 25:14-30. Substantial returns can be obtained through real estate investment as a result of appreciation in property value, income from rental property, and favorable tax treatment. The tangibility of real estate is a significant component that contributes to its attractiveness. Properties, in contrast to stocks and bonds, are tangible assets that you can see, touch, and even change; they are your very own promised land. You are able to investigate the foundation of your investment, see what it looks like on the inside, and see what it could become (Proverbs 24:3–4). This palpable reality often gives rise to a sense of safety that is consistent with the reassurance that God has given to us (Hebrews 13:5).

In addition to this, investing in real estate provides you, the investor, a level of control that cannot be found in any other financial field. You have the ability to increase the value of your property by making improvements and practicing strategic management, which exemplifies the stewardship principle found in the Bible (Luke 16:10-12).

The stability of real estate is one more quality that appeals to prospective investors. Real estate markets, much like religious beliefs, experience periods of ups and downs, but on the whole, they increase in value through time, mirroring the unchanging nature of God's love. Your money will be protected from the effects of inflation thanks to this buffer, just as we are protected by God.

Leveraging, which refers to the practice of financing a large property with a small quantity of one's own money, is a realistic approach in the real estate industry that offers the possibility of considerable returns. It is similar to how Jesus fed a large crowd with only five loaves of bread and two fish, which demonstrates the enormous potential that may come from humble beginnings (Matthew 14:13-21).

Last but not least, investing in real estate is not merely a means to amass wealth; rather, it is also a path to one's own personal fulfillment and a way to be a blessing to others. The delight that it offers is a reflection of the joy that comes from serving Christ (Galatians 5:13). This can be seen in the transformation of a derelict home into a lovely dwelling, or in the provision of quality housing.

The wisdom of some of the most well-known Christian investors in history is contained within this book, and their words will act as enlightening guiding lights as you read them.

Keep in mind that investing in real estate is not a way to become wealthy overnight. Because it is an endeavor with a long time horizon, it takes patience, smart planning, and a heart that is rooted in the teachings of Christ (Proverbs 21:5). We are happy to have you join us on this adventure, and we wish for you to find in it rewards that go beyond monetary gain.

Why Should You Put Your Money in Real Estate? - Management of Resources and the Generation of Wealth from a Christian Perspective

Real estate provides a solid and dependable vessel for you to navigate toward your goals of responsible financial management and wealth accumulation. The biblical precepts of diligence (Proverbs 22:29), stewardship (Luke 16:10-12), and multiplication (Matthew 25:14-30) are all encapsulated in the path of investing in real estate as a physical and practical investment vehicle. In this article, we will explore the compelling reasons why, from a Christian perspective, real estate should constitute a significant component of your financial portfolio:

The consistent flow of rental revenue from real estate is analogous to the daily manna that God provided for the Israelites (Exodus 16). This metaphor extends beyond the literal meaning of the term "daily bread." You are freed from the constraints of a conventional work and given the ability to serve God and your community in a more meaningful way as a result of this steady stream of income. As King Solomon so astutely explains in Proverbs 13:22, "A good person leaves an inheritance for their children's children," and the consistent rental income from your real estate assets will help you achieve this goal of leaving an inheritance.

Increase in value over time: this is what we mean when we talk about appreciation. Much like faith, the value of real estate increases through time. This is a theory that may be shown by the example of successful investors such as Barbara Corcoran, who parlayed a loan of $1,000 into a real estate empire worth $5 billion. This is similar to the parable of the mustard seed that is found in Matthew 13:31-32, in which a small seed (representing an investment) can blossom into a gigantic tree (representing a portfolio).

The multiplication of the loaves and fishes in Matthew 14:13-21 is a parable that illustrates the power of leverage. Leverage in real estate allows you to control a much larger asset with a lot smaller down payment. This parable is found in Matthew

14. Robert Kiyosaki, the renowned author of "Rich Dad Poor Dad," built a big real estate empire from tiny starting investments by applying this approach throughout his life and writing career. "Rich Dad Poor Dad" is one of the most popular personal finance books of all time.

Tax Benefits: Render Unto Caesar The tax deductions that are available to landlords have the potential to considerably boost the profitability of an investor's investments over the long term. As it is written in Deuteronomy 28:8, "The LORD will command the blessing on you in your barns and in all that you undertake." By leveraging these advantages, we uphold the biblical principle of stewardship, ensuring that what belongs to God continues to belong to God, and what belongs to Caesar is rendered unto him (Matthew 22:21).

When it comes to investing, diversification is analogous to the diverse but unified body of Christ (1 Corinthians 12:12). Adding real estate to your portfolio creates balance and lowers risk, much like how the body of Christ is diverse yet still one. Your wealth can be protected from the unpredictability of market changes if you buy properties in a variety of areas and types. This strategy is reminiscent of the sound advice found in Ecclesiastes 11:2: "Divide your investments among many places, for you do not know what risks might lie ahead."

Investing in real estate can provide some protection from the eroding effects that inflation can have on one's purchasing power. The Lord is My Shield. Real estate protects your wealth, allowing it to retain its purchasing power even while the cost of living continues to rise (Psalm 91:2), much as God is described as being our refuge and fortress in the Bible. Control: Putting the Dominion Mandate into Action When it comes to real estate, you have complete dominion over your investment, which allows you to have an immediate impact on how well it does. This echoes the command given in Genesis 1:28 to exercise stewardship over the planet and to have dominion over it. This idea is best shown by the life of Dottie Herman, a woman who raised her children by herself and rose to prominence in the field of real estate. She used the power of strategic control to turn real estate brokerage firms into a thriving empire. Her success demonstrates the power of strategic control.

The process of investing in real estate is more than just about financial returns; it is also a tangible representation of God's faithfulness and provision in our lives. Similar to the biblical account of Joseph's ascent to power in Egypt (Genesis 41:39–41), it has played a significant role in the transformation of people's lives. Through wise management of their real estate holdings, regular people like Dottie Herman and Chad Carson have been able to scale amazing heights in their careers. You are not only safeguarding your financial future as you set out on this path; you are also shaping it via responsible stewardship and astute investing, both of which have their foundations firmly planted in biblical precepts. Beginning now is important because the Bible says that "whoever can be trusted with very little can also be trusted with much" (Luke 16:10). Your way to financial success is waiting for you, and it is built on the unshakeable rock of God's Word and His promises.

Several Distinct Categories of Investments in Real Estate

Comparing entering the world of real estate investing to the Israelites' entry into the Promised Land (Joshua 1:1-9), the similarities are striking. There are a lot of different regions to discover, and each one has its own set of benefits, difficulties, and responsibilities that come with it. Let us investigate these several avenues of real estate investing further, gaining an understanding of them within the context of our religion and the word of God.

Houses, apartments, townhouses, and vacation homes are all examples of residential properties that have the potential to be lucrative investments. Residential real estate also provides us with a safe haven. They are a reflection of the biblical value of a house as a sanctuary of safety and protection (Psalm 91:1-2). When you invest in residential real estate, you are not just making a financial investment; you are also meeting a basic requirement of other people by providing them with a place to call home.

Investing in commercial assets like office buildings, retail spaces, and warehouses, among other types of commercial real estate, requires a higher level of engagement and understanding than investing in residential real estate. Our talents can be multiplied by investing in commercial real estate. However, it also results in greater rewards, much like the parable described in Matthew 25:14-30 concerning the talents. Because we are stewards of the resources that God has given us, we have the responsibility to increase what He has given us, and investing in commercial real estate provides a platform that allows us to accomplish just that.

Warehouses, factories, and distribution hubs are all examples of industrial real estate, which exemplifies the biblical principle of laboring diligently in the vineyard (Proverbs 14:23). Industrial real estate can be thought of as "laboring in the vineyard." Industrial assets play an important part in our economy and provide interesting chances for investment since they make the operations of manufacturing and distribution easier to carry out.

Raw Land Is Like Sowing a Seed and Waiting for It to Bear Fruit The act of investing in raw land is analogous to planting a seed and then waiting for it to produce fruit (Mark 4:26-29). It is necessary to have patience, a clear vision, and frequently an investment of a large amount of time. However, similar to a seed that germinates into a plant that is abundant in its harvest, undeveloped property possesses enormous promise for those who are prepared to navigate the development process.

Individuals now have the opportunity to engage in large-scale, income-generating real estate through indirect means thanks to Real Estate Investment Trusts (REITs), which bring together many investors into a single pool. This collaborative strategy is reminiscent of the early Christian community in Acts 2:44-45, which pooled their resources to have a greater impact on the world. Because they eliminate the requirement for direct administration, real estate investment trusts (REITs) allow a greater number of people to take part in expansive real estate ventures.

Keep in mind that every type of real estate investment replicates a biblical value, whether it be the provision of a place to live, the development of one's skills, the fruit of conscientious labor, the planting of the seeds of potential, or the pooling of resources to support a common goal. Pray for wisdom (James 1:5) while you investigate these potential avenues so that you can determine which one is most compatible with your calling, resources, and God-given gifts. Your trip in the world of investments should be directed by faith, wisdom, and good advice (Proverbs 15:22). Step confidently into the land of promise that is offered by the real estate investment market.

"The Blessings and Challenges of Real Estate Investment - Walking the Path of Wise Stewardship" "Separating the Wheat from the Tares: Discerning the Good Investments from the Bad"

In order to be good stewards of the resources that God has entrusted to us, we need to have an understanding of the potentials (the wheat) and the challenges (the tares) that lie within the realm of real estate investment. This concept is a reflection of Jesus' parable of the wheat and the tares, which can be found in Matthew 13:24-30.

The Favors Received - Taking Part in the Harvest of Our Labor:

Cash Flow Stability The Bible says in Proverbs 12:11, "He who tills his land will have plenty of bread." In the same way, investing in rental property can give a steady stream of income, which can either complement your current earnings or become your primary source of income.

Appreciation: The parable of the mustard seed, which is found in Matthew 13:31-32, reminds us how something small may develop greatly over time. Real estate mimics this principle, with properties often appreciating over the years, leading to huge gains when they are sold.

Tax Advantages: In the same way that God provides for His people, the tax deductions that are related with real estate investments offer monetary relief and make it possible for more effective wealth growth and maintenance.

Diversification: The book of Ecclesiastes tells us in verse 2 to "Divide your investments among many places, for you do not know what risks might lie ahead." Adding real estate to your portfolio is one way to diversify it and reduce the overall risk. Inflation Hedge: Similar to how Joseph prudently managed Egypt's resources during seven years of plenty in preparation for seven years of famine (Genesis 41), investing in real estate can be a hedge against inflation, allowing you to keep the purchasing power of your wealth intact.

When it comes to real estate, a modest down payment can control a huge property, which allows for an amplified return on investment. The Parable of the Talents, which is found in Matthew 25:14-30, advises us to make good use of the resources that we have. Leverage.

The Obstacles to Overcome and Negotiating the Rocky Road:

Liquidity: Unlike the miracle of Jesus feeding the five thousand in which resources were multiplied fast (Matthew 14:13-21), real estate investments do not become instantly liquid, and the sale of a property may take some time.

The requirements of management are similar to those placed on the diligent ant in Proverbs 6:6-8; maintaining real estate investments involves labor and insight. These requirements can include the administration of tenants and property maintenance.

Jesus tells us to expect storms in life (Matthew 7:24-27), which might be compared to the potential instability in the real estate market. Economic trends, changes in local demographics, and property oversupply can all have an effect on property values.

High Initial Expenses The parable of the pearl of great price, which is found in Matthew 13:45–46, serves to educate us that successful investments may involve high initial expenses. However, these prices may be reduced through the use of tactics such as partnership investments, real estate syndication, or crowdfunding platforms.

The parable of the rich fool, which may be found in Luke 12:13–21, serves as a cautionary tale about the unreliability of earthly money. Similarly, investing in real estate includes the danger of loss due to reasons such as market downturns, property damage, or vacancies.

Interest Rate Exposure: Just as Joseph interpreted Pharaoh's dream about the seven fat cows and the seven lean cows (Genesis 41), we must anticipate and plan for potential changes, including swings in interest rates. This is similar to how Joseph interpreted Pharaoh's dream about the seven fat cows and the seven lean cows.

We are called to be good stewards of our resources, just as the servants in the Parable of the Talents were. By having an accurate understanding of the advantages and disadvantages of real estate investment, we are able to make investments with faith, wisdom, and discernment, separating the wheat from the tares in order to produce a plentiful harvest for the glory of God.

When Choosing Your Investment Strategy, Let the Lamp of Wisdom and Diversified Stewardship Be Your Companions.

In Proverbs 24:3-4, King Solomon, the wisest man who ever lived, said, "By wisdom a house is built, and through understanding it is established; through knowledge its rooms are filled with rare and beautiful treasures." This wisdom is just as applicable to building our houses as it is to building our financial portfolios. Accordingly, as we consider various paths towards building wealth, we must strive for understanding and knowledge, recognizing that each investment vehicle has its own unique characteristics.

Real Estate: Much like the parable of the wise builder found in Matthew 7:24-27, real estate offers tangible assets that withstand the test of time. It offers the opportunity for steady rental income, capital appreciation, and significant tax advantages. Furthermore, investors have direct control over their investments, reminiscent of the good steward found in Luke 12:42. Despite these benefits, real estate requires substantial capital, ongoing management, and it is not as liquid as some other investments.

Stocks: Investing in stocks can be compared to the parable of the mustard seed found in Matthew 13:31-32, in which a small seed can grow into a large tree. Stocks, which represent ownership in a company, provide opportunities for high returns, especially in growing sectors or successful companies. They offer high liquidity and don't require management like real estate does. However, just as the seed may sometimes fail to sprout, so too can stocks carry a high degree of risk, with potential for significant losses.

Bonds: Bonds are similar to the parable of the talents found in Matthew 25:14-30, in which the servant who received one talent went and buried it in the ground to keep it safe. Bonds are relatively low-risk investments that provide fixed income over a certain period of time and preserve capital. However, bonds offer lower potential returns compared to stocks or real estate and can be impacted by fluctuations in interest rates.

Mutual funds and exchange-traded funds (ETFs): Investing in these is similar to being a part of the early Christian community (Acts 2:44-45), in which resources were pooled together. These investments provide investors with instant diversification, reducing the risk associated with investing in a single company or sector. These investments are managed by professionals and are relatively easy to buy and sell. On the other hand, they come with management fees and offer less control over individual investments compared to direct stock or

r

They offer the potential for high returns and easy cross-border transactions, serving as a hedge against the instability of traditional financial markets. However, like new wine, they are extremely volatile and speculative, and their acceptance as a payment medium is still evolving. The parable of the new wine in old wineskins can be found in Luke 5:36-38.

Cryptocurrencies represent a new form of investment. Real estate stands out for its consistent income generation, potential for appreciation, and the direct control it offers. However, success in any investment venture, as in our walk with Christ, comes from understanding the landscape, assessing your risk tolerance, diversifying your stewardship, and remaining patient and disciplined. Real estate stands out for its steady income generation, potential for appreciation, and the direct control it offers.

In all of these, let us remember the sound advice that is found in Proverbs 15:22, which states, "Plans fail for lack of counsel, but with many advisers, they succeed." Accordingly, consulting with a Christian financial advisor to guide your investment decisions based on your personal circumstances and financial goals can prove to be extremely beneficial.

Mental State: Developing an Interest in Real Estate with Faith as the Foundation

Real estate investment, in particular, calls for an enlightened mindset that is supported by an interest in the field, mental resilience, and a perspective that is firmly rooted in faith. The impact of this mindset on your journey of investing is profound. In the realm of investing, it is critical to realize that the journey goes beyond mere financial analysis and potential gains. Your journey must be fueled by a thirst for knowledge. Drawing on the advice of Proverbs 18:15, which says, "The heart of the discerning acquires knowledge, for the ears of the wise seek it out," your journey must be fueled by a deep curiosity for the field. In the vast ocean of real estate investment, there is always something new to learn. There are innumerable resources, such as books, courses, podcasts, and seminars, that offer invaluable insights that can guide you on this path.

However, the path to successful real estate investing is not an easy one. It is littered with unanticipated challenges, such as properties that require more repairs than anticipated, tenants who pose difficulties, and markets that shift unpredictably. It is in these moments that resiliency and trust in God's plan become invaluable.

In the spirit of Ecclesiastes 3:1, which says, "There is a time for everything, and a season for every activity under the heavens," real estate investment requires a great deal of patience. The real estate industry operates on a long timeline. You may frequently find yourself waiting - for properties to increase in value, for rental income to exceed expenses, or even for the right opportunity to buy or sell.

In Proverbs 27:23, there is a parable about a shepherd who must know the condition of his flocks and herds. Similarly, investors in real estate must understand the risks associated with their investments. This understanding informs your risk tolerance, which is the emotional and financial capacity to weather potential losses and the uncertainties inherent in the investing journey.

Real estate investing also requires a visionary approach. The ability to see the potential where others might overlook it is essential. Whether it's seeing the potential in a rundown property in an up-and-coming neighborhood or envisioning a novel use for an outdated building, vision can be an empowering tool in real estate investing. Let us exercise our innate creativity and vision while being guided by God, the ultimate creator, who made us in His image according to Genesis 1:27.

Last but not least, it is essential to put one's acquired knowledge and comprehension into practice, as the sage advice of Proverbs 14:23 emphasizes: "All hard work brings a profit, but mere talk leads only to poverty." Even taking relatively insignificant actions, such as visiting potential investment properties or attending local real estate meetups, can help build momentum and bring one closer to their investment goals.

In the process of developing an interest in real estate, cultivating a mindset that is resilient, patient, risk-aware, visionary, and action-oriented forms the backbone of your journey in real estate investment. When these principles harmonize with your faith, you set the stage for a successful journey that resonates with your values and life's purpose. You prepare to build a profitable real estate portfolio while honoring God through good stewardship, service to others, and embodying the values of your faith.

Let's take a moment to reflect on the journey that we've just completed as we come to the end of our first foray into the world of real estate investing. To begin, we gained an understanding of real estate from a Biblical standpoint, illuminating the fundamental concepts that govern this field. It then became clear that investing in real estate is an act of stewardship, a potent avenue for wealth creation and financial growth that enables us to serve God's kingdom more effectively.

Going into more detail, we talked about the various kinds of real estate investments. These include residential and commercial properties, Real Estate Investment Trusts (REITs), and mortgage-backed securities. Together, these represent a spectrum of opportunities, each of which comes with its own unique set of benefits and drawbacks.

We examined the benefits and drawbacks that come with investing in real estate, drawing a metaphorical parallel to the parable of the wheat and the tares. This understanding prepares us to embrace the benefits and navigate the potential pitfalls in a wise manner. In an effort to walk the path of wise stewardship, we thought about the blessings and challenges inherent in real estate investment.

After that, we shifted our attention to the significance of taking a diversified and strategic approach to investing. To illustrate this point, we drew parallels between real estate and other investment opportunities, such as stocks, bonds, mutual funds, exchange-traded funds, and cryptocurrencies, and we emphasized the significance of diversification while drawing attention to the special place that real estate can have in a well-balanced portfolio.

Our faith, which is firmly rooted in Christian values, serves as a guiding light on our investment journey, shaping both our decisions and our approach. Finally, we delved into the mental aspects of investing, highlighting the importance of interest, resilience, patience, understanding of risk, and vision in real estate investment.

As we've seen, investing in real estate involves much more than financial decisions; rather, it's an act of faithful stewardship that ought to reflect our Christian values and serve God's purpose. In conclusion, this investigation has laid a solid foundation for understanding real estate investing from a Biblical perspective.

Having examined these topics, let us now consolidate our understanding and focus on how these insights could apply to our personal life and financial goals. This can be accomplished by prayer, thought, and making goals that are both realistic and based on faith.

When you pray, ask for wisdom and discernment to comprehend these concepts and how they apply to your stewardship obligations. During the next week, schedule a quiet time each day to pray and contemplate on the insights that have been acquired.

Next, after each time you pray and think, write down any thoughts, questions, and personal applications that come to mind in a journal. The purpose of this step is not to make a flawless account, but rather to let you to digest and record your insights on paper.

After this, you should determine a goal for real estate investment that is attainable, quantifiable, and in line with your personal financial situation, level of risk tolerance, and faith-guided investment strategy for the coming year. This goal could involve learning more about real estate, setting aside a certain amount of money for a down payment, or even buying your first investment property.

As a final step, after you have established your objective, pray a prayer of commitment, in which you ask God to direct your steps, give you wisdom, and assist you in remaining committed as you work towards achieving your objective. Keep in mind that the purpose of this exercise is not solely to gain financial gain, but rather to learn how to effectively steward your resources for the glory of God.

Real estate investing is more like running a marathon than a sprint; it calls for consistent forward movement, patience, and self-control. Although the journey may initially appear difficult, keep in mind that through prayer, reflection, and action, you can make progress toward your financial goals and become a wise steward of the resources God has entrusted to you. May God bless you on your journey!

The Real Estate Market and Financial Literacy

The capacity to comprehend and apply various financial skills, such as personal financial management, budgeting, and investing, is an essential component of any real estate plan. Financial literacy is the ability to understand and use these abilities. When Christians are armed with this knowledge, they are better prepared to make decisions that are in line with the ideals of their faith while also efficiently managing and expanding their resources.

When it comes to dealing with issues related to money, the Bible exhorts believers to be knowledgeable and prudent. It is written that "by wisdom a house is built, and through understanding it is established; through knowledge its rooms are filled with rare and beautiful treasures." These verses may be found in Proverbs 24:3-4. This idea relates to both our actual homes as well as our financial situations, highlighting the significance of increasing our level of financial literacy.

Personal Financial Management

Management of one's own personal finances is the cornerstone of sound financial education. This competency requires knowledge of how to handle one's own personal finances, including one's income, expenses, savings, and any outstanding debt. The Bible provides helpful instruction on these subjects, such as the significance of putting money aside (Proverbs 6:6-8), staying away from debt (Proverbs 22:7), and learning to be happy with what one possesses (Hebrews 13:5).

Budgeting

Creating a budget is an essential part of managing one's own finances. It entails formulating a strategy for how you will spend your money on a monthly basis, with the intention of ensuring that you have sufficient funds for essentials, savings, and other monetary objectives. In Luke 14:28, Jesus Himself brought attention to the significance of establishing a financial plan by saying, "Suppose one of you wants to construct a tower. Will you first take a seat and make an estimate of the cost to determine whether or not you have sufficient funds to finish it?

Investing

Another essential component of financial literacy is the ability to invest, particularly in the context of the real estate market. Jesus shows us the significance of investing and developing our riches rather than merely putting them away in the "Parable of the Talents" found in Matthew 25:14-30. This parable is found in Matthew. It is essential to have a solid understanding of the fundamentals of investing, such as the dynamic that exists between risk and return, the value of diversification, and the role that time plays in the process.

Specifics Regarding Real Estate

When it comes to real estate, having a solid awareness of the real estate market, the various financing choices, and the costs associated with purchasing and selling properties is an essential component of having a solid financial literacy. It is also extremely important to have a solid understanding of the long-term financial ramifications of owning a piece of real estate, such as the continuous costs of things like property taxes, maintenance, and other fees associated with homeowner's associations.

To be financially literate, one must not only comprehend the aforementioned ideas but also put them into practice in a way that is consistent with one's religious beliefs. For instance, although though the Bible does not directly address credit ratings, keeping a good credit score can be seen as demonstrating that one acts with integrity and honors their obligations, both of which are values that are emphasized throughout the Bible (Psalm 15:4).

The purpose of this endeavor is not to amass fortune for its own sake, but rather to put that wealth to work honoring God and helping other people. As our knowledge of finance expands, we should keep in mind the importance of praying for God's direction, putting our faith in His ability to provide for us, and blessing the lives of others by making investments not only in real estate but also in the advancement of the kingdom of God.

Gaining an Understanding of Christian Perspectives on Real Estate and Finance

As Christians, we have been given the responsibility of stewarding the resources and money that God has entrusted to us in a manner that brings glory to Him. A desire to serve God and make good use of these riches ought to be the driving force behind financial management and investment decisions, rather than the pursuit of profit alone. "We are just the managers of the inheritance God has given to us," David Green, the founder of Hobby Lobby and author of "Giving It All Away...and Getting It All Back Again: The Way of Living Generously," claims.

In Psalms 24:1, it is said that "the earth is the Lord's, and everything in it, the world, and all who live in it." This verse serves to remind us that "the earth is the Lord's, and everything in it." This scripture emphasizes once again that God is the rightful owner of everything we possess, including our money and our possessions. We are only managers of the assets that belong to him.

There is a wealth of financial advice to be found in the Bible. In the book of Proverbs, chapter 22, verse 7, it says that "the rich rule over the poor, and the borrower is a slave to the lender." This passage encourages people to stay away from undue debt, which is a fundamental practice important for achieving monetary success. In addition, Ecclesiastes 5:10-11 cautions against falling in love with luxury and money because it can never truly fulfill. Instead, we ought to center our attention on putting our wealth to use in the service of God and other people.

In this sense, having a solid awareness of and commitment to the upkeep of our credit ratings constitutes a vital component of responsible financial management. Dave Ramsey, a well-known Christian financial advisor, emphasizes in his book "Financial Peace Revisited" that a person's credit score does not indicate whether or not they would be successful financially. The only thing it can tell you is whether or not you have a good track record of borrowing money and repaying it. Because having a high credit score can affect our ability to obtain loans, rent apartments, and even find employment, it is a clear indicator of our financial responsibility. Having a good credit score can affect our ability to gain loans, rent apartments, and even find jobs.

The Basic Concept Behind Cash-Out Refinancing

It is essential to have a solid understanding of particular financial methods, such as cash out refinance. This method of obtaining a mortgage enables you to take out a loan against the equity in your home, which can provide funding for a variety of purposes, including higher education, business endeavors, and home renovation projects. The prudent perceive danger and seek refuge, but the simple keep going and pay the penalty; therefore, we must be careful not to borrow more than we can afford. This is in accordance with Proverbs 22:3, which states, "The simple keep going and pay the penalty."

An Examination of Real Estate Investing from a Christian Standpoint

Putting money into real estate can be one of the most effective methods to acquire wealth; yet, this endeavor requires caution and should always be approached with gratitude for God's providence. According to Jim Pappas, a well-known Christian real estate investor and author of the book "Real Estate Investing God's Way," "Real estate is a God-given asset that produces income." Be respectful to it, and in whatever that you do, honor the Lord with your investments.

When it comes to investing in real estate, we are commanded to put our faith in God's provision, pray for His direction, and take steps to safeguard our interests. Matthew chapter 6 verses 31-33 gives us assurance of God's provision for us: "Therefore, you need not be concerned, saying things like, 'What shall we eat?' or 'What shall we drink?' or 'What shall we wear?'...But seek first his kingdom and his righteousness, and all these other things, including life, liberty, and the pursuit of happiness, will be given to you.

Choosing Wisely Among Available Mortgage Programs

Real estate requires a certain level of financial literacy, one component of which is an understanding of the various mortgage alternatives. Mortgages with fixed rates, adjustable rates, FHA mortgages, VA mortgages, or conventional mortgages are all choices that should be made after careful consideration, prayer, and advice from others. The Bible's

Proverbs chapter 15 verse 22 reads that "Plans fail for lack of counsel, but with many advisers they succeed."

In conclusion, having a Christian worldview when it comes to understanding financial and real estate requires having insight, practicing good stewardship, and having faith in God's provision. We are not only asked to make investments in the temporal realm, but we are also invited to make investments in the eternal realm by utilizing our resources to further the cause of God's kingdom here on earth.

The Importance of Placing Your Trust in God's Provision When Financing Your Real Estate Investment

The financing of a real estate transaction typically requires a significant amount of money and comes with a variety of obstacles to overcome. However, as Christians, we are aware that every blessing, including our financial resources, comes from God (James 1:17). This holds true regardless of the nature of the blessing.

If we put our faith in God to guide our decisions with our finances, including our investments in real estate, this does not mean that we should make no effort or fail to give careful consideration to our options. Dave Ramsey encourages his readers in his book "Total Money Makeover" to "pray like it all depends on God, but work like it all depends on you." This exemplifies the delicate balancing act that must be performed between placing one's trust in divine direction and accepting individual accountability for one's actions.

Our requests for direction ought to be accompanied by careful investigation and an in-depth comprehension of the real estate market, available mortgage programs, current interest rates, and the long-term ramifications of such a substantial financial commitment. In the book of Proverbs chapter 24 verses 3 and 4, the Bible teaches us that "by wisdom a house is built, and through understanding, it is established; through knowledge, its rooms are filled with rare and beautiful treasures."

In addition, keep in mind that God can direct our steps in a variety of ways, including directly through His Word, through the counsel of godly counselors, or through the circumstances themselves. Because we have shown that we are willing to surrender to God's will, we can have peace with the decisions that we have made if we seek the wisdom of God.

Examining Various Mortgage Options While Keeping an Open Mind

Because of the influence that this decision will have on our finances, choose the right mortgage plan is one of the most important aspects of investing in real estate. In this perspective, wisdom is not only worldly information but rather an insight that is anchored in the principles that God has established.

According to Proverbs 2:6-7, we learn that "For the Lord gives wisdom; from his mouth come knowledge and understanding; he stores up sound wisdom for the upright; he is a shield to those who walk in integrity." When contemplating the various possibilities for our mortgage, we should seek this kind of advice.

Mortgages can come with a variety of terms and conditions, such as fixed rates, adjustable rates, FHA loans, VA loans, or conventional loans. Each one comes with its own set of conditions, rates, advantages, and disadvantages. To be able to make a decision that is based on accurate information, we need to perform our due diligence, conduct study on each possibility, and consult with financial experts, especially those who acknowledge the lordship of Christ and base their advice on biblical principles.

Luke 14:28 is another passage that brings this principle to our attention. It asks, "For which of you, intending to build a tower, does not first sit down and estimate the cost, to see whether he has enough to complete it?" By carefully considering all of the associated expenses as well as the possibility of future changes in interest rates, we can stay true to the teachings of God and avoid entering into a financial commitment that we will be unable to uphold.

The cultivation of a financially disciplined mindset in accordance with the principles of the Bible.

When it comes to making judgments about money, our state of mind is quite important. It is the beginning of self-discipline. The ability to think in a disciplined manner leads to behavior that is disciplined, which is essential for responsible financial management. As followers of Christ, the Bible imparts upon us ideas that, when put into practice, result in monetary self-control and, as a corollary, monetary tranquility.

The development of sound financial habits is more of a long-term endeavor than a quick fix. It requires making sound decisions on a constant basis, such as living within our means, avoiding taking on excessive debt, saving, investing intelligently, and giving generously. These deeds give credence to the words of wisdom found in Proverbs 13:11, which state, "Dishonest money dwindles away, but whoever gathers money little by little makes it grow."

In his book "Your Money Counts," Howard Dayton highlights that "God's way of handling money is contrary to the world's way." [Citation needed] Dayton's words are taken from the book. The biblical precepts instruct us to be satisfied even in the face of society's pressure to pursue materialism and instant gratification, but society continues to push us in those directions.

In 1 Timothy chapter six verse ten, the apostle Paul pens the following: "For the love of money is a root of all kinds of evil." In their pursuit of wealth, several individuals have strayed from the true faith and caused themselves untold suffering as a result. This exemplifies the possible peril of placing an undue focus on monetary success. Therefore, keeping our attention focused on the teachings that Christ gave us helps us create the appropriate attitude when it comes to money.

The Real Estate Market

Understanding Market Trends through the Lens of Faith

This chapter delves into the fascinating dynamics of the real estate market and how a believer can navigate this territory. An understanding of real estate trends is vital, but equally important is the application of faith-based principles in our approach.

It may seem like an impossible undertaking, but for a wise real estate investor, understanding the development potential of diverse areas is an essential component of the journey. It is necessary to do a thorough investigation of population shifts, conduct an analysis of available employment prospects, and pay close attention to the development of infrastructure. Even if it's a complicated procedure, we don't carry it out by ourselves. As Christians, we are constantly reminded of the heavenly knowledge and direction that is at our disposal.

In the book of Proverbs chapter 3, verses 5 and 6, the Bible instructs us to "Trust in the Lord with all your heart, and do not lean on your own understanding; in all your ways, submit to him, and he will make your paths straight." The knowledge of our Lord is beyond our ability to comprehend, and He has a predetermined plan for everything that happens on earth, including the expansion and development of its cities and towns.

In his book "The Millionaire Real Estate Investor," well-known Christian investor Gary Keller places a strong emphasis on the significance of the divine order in relation to his business techniques. He says, "My achievement is not the result of random chance. It is by divine design, and if you line your methods with His intentions, it can also be by divine design for you if you so choose.

How therefore can those of us who call ourselves Christians bring our financial plans into alignment with His divine purposes? It all starts with careful consideration and in-depth study. It is necessary for us to keep an eye on the demographic shifts that are taking place in potential markets. Opportunities for real estate investors can frequently be found in regions that are experiencing population increase, particularly if the population is getting younger.

The creation of new jobs is yet another essential component. There will most certainly be a need for housing in areas that are luring new firms and industries to the area, which will result in the creation of new job possibilities. The construction of essential infrastructure is another indication of a potential for market expansion. An increase in the quality of the area's public facilities, as well as its transportation and utility systems, makes it more appealing to both inhabitants and companies.

However, the findings of this research and analysis represent only a single variable in the equation. As Christians who invest, we have an additional responsibility to supplement our conclusions with prayer and self-examination. According to the words that are written in James 1:5, "If any of you lacks wisdom, you should ask God, who gives generously to all without finding fault, and it will be given to you." We can align ourselves with God's divine plan and ensure that our investments not only bring financial rewards but also honor and glorify Him by seeking the knowledge of God in our financial decisions and seeking to follow His will.

Therefore, when we delve into the complexities of locating growing markets, let us do so with the word of God as our guide and have faith in His omniscient knowledge to lead us to profitable investments. After all, the plans that the Lord has for us are always intended to bring us success, and having faith in the Lord's understanding is essential to maximizing the potential of our real estate investment strategy.

The Impact of Economic Factors on Real Estate: Trusting in God's Sovereignty

The real estate market is heavily impacted by a wide range of economic factors, such as prevailing inflation and interest rates as well as the overall trajectory of economic expansion. Having an understanding of these factors and the effect they have on the market can significantly improve our capacity to make well-informed investing decisions. However, the unpredictability and volatility of these circumstances serve as a powerful reminder of God's omnipotent control and sovereignty over everything, even the economic systems of the world that we live in.

When it comes to the affordability of mortgages and the value of real estate investments, economic factors like rates of inflation and interest rates play a significant influence in the decision-making process. For instance, increased inflation typically results in higher interest rates, which can result in higher mortgage costs and a decrease in the market for real estate. On the other hand, periods of economic growth tend to promote the housing market. This is because job security and rising incomes make home ownership more attainable for a greater number of persons during times of economic expansion.

It is crucial for us to be aware of these elements and take them into consideration when making decisions about our investments. Nevertheless, as Christians, we acknowledge that despite our best attempts to comprehend and forecast the state of the economy, uncertainty will always be a part of our lives as long as we are physically present in this world. These economic forces, which are prone to undergoing sudden shifts, have the potential to render ineffectual even the most meticulously crafted programs.

During times like this, we are commanded to place our trust in the omnipotence of God. We are prompted to remember this truth in Proverbs 19:21, which states, "Many are the plans in a person's heart, but it is the purpose of the LORD that prevails." This verse demonstrates that God's will is more important than any of our own plans that we may have. Even in the sphere of finance and investments in real estate, the results are ultimately decided by Him alone.

Dave Ramsey, a Christian investor, writes in his book "Financial Peace Revisited" that the "secret to success in handling money is to devise a plan that is faithful to the scripture and then work that plan with all of your heart." Ramsey says that this is the "secret to success in handling money." Due to the ever-evolving nature of life's circumstances, it is inevitable that this plan will be altered on occasion. Nevertheless, despite of the changes that take place in your life, you should never give up on the fundamental stewardship principles that God puts out in His Word.

As a result, we put our faith in God's wisdom in order to guide us through the unpredictability of the current economic climate. We are aware that even though we can make plans and devise strategies, the ultimate consequences are ultimately under God's authority. The role that we are called to play as devout investors is to prudently and responsibly manage our money while placing our confidence in the divine providence of God. This conviction releases us from concern and enables us to make decisions regarding our investments with confidence rather than fear.

Let us not forget to put our faith in the omnipotence of God as we negotiate the consequences that a variety of economic issues have on the real estate market. Our success will not depend on our capacity to divine the future; rather, it will result from our unwavering commitment to being good stewards of the resources that God has given us and from our unwavering faith in His all-encompassing authority over everything.

Risks and How to Mitigate Them: Walking by Faith, Not by Sight

There is always some degree of danger associated with any investment you make, and real estate is no exception. Market volatility, property depreciation, unforeseen expenses, and increases in interest rates are some of the most prevalent dangers associated with investing in the real estate market.

However, by being aware of these dangers and coming up with plans to eliminate or reduce them, we can considerably increase the likelihood that we will be successful in the real estate market.

Every investment is subject to the risk of the market being volatile. Prices may shift for a variety of reasons, including the state of the economy, shifts in the labor market, and modifications to relevant policies. Depreciation of a property is another risk that arises when the value of a property drops over time as a consequence of factors such as the property's physical deterioration or changes in the surrounding neighborhood. Unanticipated costs, such as those for pricey repairs or legal troubles, might create major difficulties for one's finances. In addition, a rise in interest rates may result in higher monthly mortgage payments, which in turn may reduce the profitability of investment properties.

A comprehensive market study, routine property maintenance, setting aside emergency cash for unanticipated costs, and locking in a fixed-rate mortgage as a protection against interest rate hikes are all strategies that can be used to lessen the dangers associated with this situation. Despite the fact that these precautions have been taken, it is impossible to ignore the fact that danger still exists.

At this juncture, our Christian faith must step forward and take center stage. When we decide to invest in real estate, we do it with the knowledge that we are not walking by sight but rather by faith. This is important to us. According to the verse in 2 Corinthians chapter 5 verse 7, "For we live by faith, not by sight." Even in the face of unpredictability and the possibility of being set back, we put our faith in the providence and guidance of God.

"Faith is taking the first step even when you don't see the whole staircase," Robert Kiyosaki, a Christian and the author of "Rich Dad, Poor Dad," emphasizes. This encapsulates the core of our strategy for the control of risks associated with real estate investment. We knowingly put ourselves in harm's way, but we do it with an unshakable confidence that God is in charge.

In the end, we put our faith and reliance not in our plans, our findings, or our predictions, but in God. Even if we can't get rid of all hazards, we can lessen their impact by being responsible with how we manage our money. In addition, we do not approach these dangers with fear, but rather with the assurance that God is with us and will lead us along the route that He has laid out for us. Let us keep in mind the words of Proverbs 3:5-6 as we deliberate and go forward in the process of purchasing real estate: "Trust in the Lord with all your heart, and do not lean on your own understanding; in all your ways submit to him, and he will make your paths straight."

We are not paralyzed by dread of what may come, but rather are motivated by confidence in God's sovereign purpose as we manage the complexity and uncertainties of the real estate market. We navigate these challenges by combining tactical solutions with unwavering faith.

Mental State: Being Comfortable with Uncertainty through Faith

The volatility and unpredictability of the real estate market can, in fact, be a cause of stress and anxiety for those who are involved in it. On the other hand, the fact that we are Christians enables us to view these difficulties through a perspective that is wholly unique. We don't have to let the unknowns cause us to feel overwhelmed; rather, we can discover serenity, comfort, and even progress in the midst of them.

According to Philippians 4:6-7, "Do not be anxious about anything, but in every situation, present your requests to God by praying and petitioning with thanksgiving." And the peace of God, which surpasses all comprehension, will protect your hearts and your minds in the name of Jesus Christ. These verses serve as a reminder that we can take all of our concerns to God in prayer, including those that are related to the investments we have made in real estate.

In addition, the book of James tells us in verses 2 through 4: "Consider it pure joy, my brothers and sisters, whenever you face trials of many kinds, because you know that the testing of your faith produces perseverance. " Perseverance should be allowed to accomplish its work so that you can become mature and whole, without anything being missing. These tests, particularly the tests that come with investment, have the potential to be used to fortify our faith and our character.

"Fear is the enemy of hope," is a quote attributed to Dave Ramsey, a well-known Christian financial planner and author. Fear, however, is not a fruit that comes from the spirit. The emotion of fear is not a sound financial strategy. The three virtues of faith, hope, and love are a sound investment strategy. Because of our faith, we are able to fearlessly confront the unknown, because we are aware that our hope does not lie in the ever-changing market, but rather in our God, who does not change.

In the midst of the unpredictability of the market, it is necessary to continually draw on our faith and seek God's wisdom in order to keep a positive mental state. It is essential to have an up-to-date knowledge base and to be well-prepared for any potential shifts in the market; yet, it is equally essential to place your faith in the authority and timing of God. Let us always keep in mind the words of Proverbs 16:9 as we move forward in the process of navigating the real estate market: "In their hearts humans plan their course, but the Lord establishes their steps." We can devise our strategies and perform the research that is required of us, but in the end, we put our faith in God to direct our steps and look out for what is in our best interests.

Being at ease with ambiguity does not imply a disregard for potential threats or an inability to make preparations for them. Instead, it implies that we go on with discernment and an unshakable faith in God's providence for our lives. It means having faith that God can turn any circumstance around to work for our benefit and for the glory of God, as promised in Romans 8:28: "And we know that in all things God works for the good of those who love him, who have been called according to his purpose." Because of our deep-seated faith, we are able to manage the chaotic world of real estate investment with calm and confidence despite its inherent uncertainty.

We have started an investigation into the world of real estate, and we will be viewing the markets through the prism of our religious beliefs. We began by locating growing markets, and then we learnt how to analyze the potential of these markets by concentrating on demographic trends, job growth, and the development of infrastructure. Our faith instructs us that God has a divine design for the entire world, and that this purpose includes the cities and towns that populate the earth. We have made it a priority to seek His counsel in order to ensure that our plans are in accordance with His desire.

The economic considerations that have an impact on the market for real estate were another topic of discussion. Because of this, we have learned that, despite the unpredictability of factors such as inflation rates, interest rates, and economic growth, we must always place our faith in God's sovereignty. Because He is in control of everything, even the final results of our goals, we should put our faith in him.

As we progressed through this trip, we were forced to confront the truth that the real estate market is fraught with risks. As Christians, our faith has instructed us to meet these unpredictabilities by walking by faith and not by sight, and to constantly rely in God's providence. This is something that we have learned to do as a result of our faith. Because of this unshakeable faith, we are able to reduce the impact of these risks and confidently go forward.

In the end, we discussed ways in which we can keep our mental health in check despite the constant shifts in the real estate market. Even when we are confronted with unpredictability in the market, we are able to find serenity because to our confidence in God's goodness and control. In the midst of the ups and downs of the real estate market, we are able to maintain our composure because to the unwavering conviction that underpins our lives.

As we get to the close of this chapter, we might take some time to consider how we've combined the teachings of the Bible with the observations of well-known Christian financial counselors. It is the harmonic combination of these two worlds that has illuminated the route for us, directing our steps towards sensible and godly investing decisions in real estate. The path has been enlightened because of the harmonious blend of these two realms. We pray that while we continue on this road, we will never waiver in our faith and that we will always allow it to serve as the compass that directs us in every choice that we make.

Buying Investment Properties

The Buying Process: Prayerful Consideration

Buying property should always be the first step in any successful real estate investment strategy. However, as we move forward with this process, it is absolutely necessary that our strategic thinking be supplemented with contemplations based on prayer. The complexities of the real estate market can at times be intimidating, which may at times cause us to feel hesitant or anxious. During times like these, it is really necessary to rely on our faith and take our concerns to God so that we can make choices that are in line with His plan.

The Bible, notably Philippians 4:6, encourages us not to give in to our worries but rather to bring all of our questions, requests, and concerns to God via prayer and thankfulness. This verse serves as a potent reminder for us not to rely entirely on our own understanding but rather to incorporate our faith and spirituality into the procedures by which we make decisions.

According to the sound advice of John Templeton, a Christian investor who specializes in real estate, "The first step to success in investment is prayer." Only God can direct us to make the best choices for ourselves and give us the serenity to carry them out. We are not only making a financial investment when we incorporate prayer into our purchasing process; rather, we are making an investment in our spiritual growth and forging a stronger relationship with God. This is an investment that is more valuable than money.

Let us continue to go on through this stage while continually seeking the counsel and insight of God. By taking a proactive prayer approach, we encourage God to participate in our financial planning, thereby creating space for divine wisdom and guidance. It is not enough to just beg God to bless our plans; rather, we must endeavor to understand what His plans are for us. In Jeremiah 29:11, the Bible tells us that "For I know the plans I have for you," says the LORD. These plans are "plans to prosper you and not to harm you, plans to give you hope and a future." Because we have this assurance in our hearts, we are able to traverse the journey of real estate investment with confidence.

Finding the Right Property: Divine Guidance

Buying property should always be the first step in any successful real estate investment strategy. However, as we move forward with this process, it is absolutely necessary that our strategic thinking be supplemented with contemplations based on prayer. The complexities of the real estate market can at times be intimidating, which may at times cause us to feel hesitant or anxious. During times like these, it is really necessary to rely on our faith and take our concerns to God so that we can make choices that are in line with His plan. Philippians 4:6, encourages us not to give in to our worries but rather to bring all of our questions, requests, and concerns to God via prayer and thankfulness. This verse serves as a potent reminder for us not to rely entirely on our own understanding but rather to incorporate our faith and spirituality into the procedures by which we make decisions. According to the sound advice of John Templeton, a Christian investor who specializes in real estate, "The first step to success in investment is prayer." Only God can direct us to make the best choices for ourselves and give us the serenity to carry them out. We are not only making a financial investment when we incorporate prayer into our purchasing process; rather, we are making an investment in our spiritual growth and forging a stronger relationship with God. This is an investment that is more valuable than money.

Let us continue to go on through this stage while continually seeking the counsel and insight of God. By taking a proactive prayer approach, we encourage God to participate in our financial planning, thereby creating space for divine wisdom and guidance. It is not enough to just beg God to bless our plans; rather, we must endeavor to understand what His plans are for us. In Jeremiah 29:11, the Bible tells us that "For I know the plans I have for you," says the LORD. These plans are "plans to prosper you and not to harm you, plans to give you hope and a future." Because we have this assurance in our hearts, we are able to traverse the journey of real estate investment with confidence.

Assessing a Property's Potential: Exercising God-given Wisdom

The evaluation of a property's potential returns on investment is one of the most important steps involved in the process of investing in real estate. This requires having an awareness of the conditions of the market, doing an assessment of the qualities of the property, and estimating its potential future value. However, as we go more into these technical components, it is essential that we recognize the role that wisdom bestowed by God plays in the process. The ability to recognize a good bargain when one is presented, the insight to anticipate possible problems, and the wisdom to make prudent decisions regarding investments are all forms of wisdom.

Dave Ramsey, a Christian financial expert, writes in his book "The Total Money Makeover," "Pray like it all depends on God, but work like it all depends on you." This advice is one of his most famous quotes. When it comes to determining the potential of a piece of real estate, this ideology encapsulates the ideal combination of heavenly insight and human endeavor. We seek God's guidance via prayer, but we also make a commitment to acting responsibly in all that we do.

It is reassuring to be reminded of this in James 1:5, which says, "If any of you lacks wisdom, you should ask God, who gives generously to all without finding fault, and it will be given to you." Therefore, when we evaluate each possible investment, let us pray to God for guidance in comprehending the numbers, making sense of the data regarding the market, and anticipating the future of the property. The information that we learn, in conjunction with the wisdom bestowed upon us by God, will act as a compass for us and lead us to make profitable investments in real estate.

However, it is crucial to keep in mind that wisdom is not just about making decisions that may result in financial gain. In addition to this, it entails making moral decisions that are consistent with our Christian beliefs. Let us make it a goal, as we go through the process of evaluating each property, to make choices that are consistent with our dedication to integrity, stewardship, and love for our neighbor.

We aren't on our own in this process of determining the possibilities of a piece of real estate. We are able to make well-informed judgments that will not only produce monetary rewards but will also bring glory to God when we are armed with data, empowered by our work, and guided by the wisdom of God. Therefore, as we embark on this journey that will test us but also reward us in the end, let us consistently pray for wisdom, work tirelessly, and put our faith in God's direction.

Making an Offer and Closing: Navigating with Integrity

Exciting and nerve-wracking are two words that may be used to describe the stage of making an offer and finalizing the sale. It is a symbol of the completion of all of the hard work that we have put in, including researching, evaluating, praying, and seeking spiritual guidance. But as we get closer to this turning point, it is of the utmost importance to keep in mind how significant it is to act with honesty and integrity at all times.

A notable Christian businessman named Larry Burkett wrote a book titled "Business by the Book," in which he reminded readers that "If you compromise in the area of integrity, you have opened a door that allows for compromise in every other area of life." It is a persuasive reminder that as Christian investors, we shouldn't let the attraction of profit lead us astray from the biblical principles that we base our investing decisions on.

When it comes to having moral rectitude, the Bible is very explicit. In the book of Proverbs, chapter 11, verse 3, it is said that "the integrity of the upright guides them, but the unfaithful are destroyed by their duplicity." In the context of the purchase or sale of real estate, this refers to conducting oneself in an open, forthright, and honorable manner throughout the process of making an offer and concluding the transaction. It is imperative that we make it a priority to provide complete transparency, maintain an attitude of open communication, and treat fairly with all parties concerned. Our behavior ought to be a demonstration of our dedication to adhering to Christian precepts, which would show that our faith permeates every facet of our lives, including the way we do business.

But preserving one's integrity isn't only about staying away from dishonest behavior; it also requires making an effort to look out for the interests of other people. Author Randy Alcorn, who identifies as a Christian, argues in his book "The Treasure Principle" that "God prospers me not to raise my standard of living but to raise my standard of giving." This frame of mind is one that we, as Christians who invest, ought to adopt. We have an obligation to make certain that the outcomes of our business dealings are beneficial not only to ourselves but also to the community and the other parties involved.

Let's make sure that every step we take on the way to making an offer and concluding the deal is guided by honesty and a commitment to acting in a manner that is fair to all parties. Through the path we are taking in real estate investing, our ultimate objective is not simply to accumulate property but to bring honor to God. Therefore, let us make it a goal to make this process a testament of our faith by acting in a way that reflects the love and justice of God in all we do.

Mental State: Patience and Perseverance in the Buying Process

The steps involved in purchasing a piece of real estate are not for those who are easily discouraged. It puts us to the test on many different levels, requiring patience, perseverance, and undivided concentration. As Christian investors, we have a responsibility to develop these characteristics and rely on our faith to sustain us through every step of this challenging path. Hannah Whitall Smith, a Christian author, said in her book "The Christian's Secret of a Happy Life" that "the true secret of giving advice is, after you have honestly given it, to be perfectly indifferent whether it is taken or not, and never persist in trying to set people right." Hannah Whitall Smith is quoted as saying that "the true secret of giving advice is, after you have honestly given it, to be perfectly indifferent whether it is taken or not." As we attempt to navigate the often turbulent seas of the housing market, the wisdom contained in this advise rings true. Even if the properties we have selected do not live up to our initial expectations or if the outcome of the talks is not what we had hoped for, we must exercise patience and continue moving forward.

Our faith has a significant bearing on our capacity for patience. The passage in Hebrews 6:12 exhorts us to "be imitators of those who through faith and patience inherit the promises." Patience is not simply the ability to wait; rather, it involves preserving a positive attitude, sustaining trust, and realizing that God's timing is being worked out even as we wait.

Additionally, perseverance is an essential quality for us to possess on this path. Transactions involving real estate typically include a number of challenges and obstacles. According to Romans 5:3-4, which serves as a helpful reminder for us, "Not only so, but we also glory in our sufferings, because we know that suffering produces perseverance; perseverance, character; and character, hope." In the midst of difficulties, we are to resist the temptation to become disheartened and instead view these tests as opportunities to develop our moral fiber and increase the breadth of our religious convictions.

Rick Warren writes in his book, "The Purpose Driven Life," that he believes that "God is more interested in your character than He is in your comfort." God is more concerned with sanctifying your life than He is with bringing you joy in your daily activities. This highlights the significance of maintaining a level of perseverance throughout the purchasing process when dealing with real estate investments. The fact that we are determined to persevere in the face of challenges reveals that we have faith in the plan and timing that God has in store for us.

In a nutshell, the process of purchasing something requires a significant amount of patience as well as perseverance. Let us not forget to be unwavering in our commitment to these admirable qualities as we proceed through this stage. Not only will they direct us toward profitable investments, but they will also mold us into the godly investors that we are meant to be. As we come to the end of this discussion, we pause to consider how the intersection of religion and practice has shaped our path toward the acquisition of investment properties. The process, which may be difficult and demanding, is made easier to navigate and more gratifying when we actively integrate our Christian beliefs with good financial principles. The procedure can be hard and demanding.

We have realized that each step of the purchasing process presents us with an opportunity to rely more heavily on our faith. The presence of God is essential to the success of our endeavor. From the very beginning, when we are guided in our choices by prayerful reflection, to the search for the ideal property, when we are actively seeking divine guidance, God is with us every step of the way. When we evaluate the possibilities of a piece of real estate, we rely on the wisdom that God has given us so that we can make the best decisions possible regarding our investments.

Integrity, patience, and perseverance are tenets that have proven useful throughout our conversation, particularly in terms of making an offer, concluding a business, and keeping a good mental state. As Christians, we make it a point to work on developing these particular virtues, and it is encouraging to see how they help us navigate the world of finance.

In addition to this, we have utilized the teachings of Christian financial consultants and authors in order to shed light on the way forward by contemplating the knowledge and understanding that these individuals have gained. Their sayings have not only contributed to an expansion of our knowledge of real estate investing, but they have also acted as timely reminders of the pertinence and applicability of our religion in all area of our life, including the financial sphere.

As we come to a close, let us not forget that our path through real estate investment is just as much a spiritual trip as it is a move that is strategically designed to increase our wealth. This presents us with the chance to put our faith into action and observe God at work in our daily lives. We have faith that the guiding principles will empower you to manage the intricacies of the purchasing process with intelligence, integrity, and faith, and that they will bring you closer to the investment goals you have set for yourself.

Moving forward, we will continue to investigate the ways in which our religion and the business of real estate investing intersect, and we will look to the Bible for direction as we delve deeper into various facets of this undertaking. Remember that the Bible tells us in Proverbs 16:3 to "Commit to the Lord whatever you do, and He will establish your plans."

Selling Investment Properties

When and Why to Sell: Discerning God's Timing

When it comes to the process of selling an investment property, it is not enough to merely focus on turning a profit; one must also have a grasp of the timing that is perfect according to God. To sell something at the right time and for the right reasons takes discernment and a close relationship to the will of God. This is not a choice that should be taken carelessly or chosen just out of the motivation to increase one's wealth. Ecclesiastes 3:1 tells us that "There is a time for everything, and a season for every activity under the heavens." This verse serves as a helpful reminder. This text exhorts us to take into consideration not only the monetary implications of our choice but also the divine timing when we make our choice.

When we are trying to figure out when the optimum moment is to sell our homes or other properties, we need to pray for direction and have faith that God has a plan. His timing is always flawless, even when it doesn't always correspond with our own expectations or wants. His time is always right. Randy Alcorn, a Christian financial planner, wrote in his book "The Treasure Principle: Unlocking the Secret of Joyful Giving," "God prospers me not to raise my standard of living, but to raise my standard of giving."

When we approach selling with this frame of mind, we don't perceive it as merely a money transaction; rather, we see it as a part of God's greater plan for our stewardship and generosity. Together with our prayerful discernment, we can gain a deeper understanding of when and why to sell by taking into consideration aspects such as the state of the market, our financial goals, and our personal circumstances.

As we proceed further into the intricate details of the selling process, let us not forget to take a breather and pray to God for direction. We are able to make choices that are both respectful to God and beneficial to ourselves if we put our faith in the fact that He is in control of all events and knows exactly when they should take place.

As we get ready to sell our properties, we feel compelled by our Christian faith to exercise exemplary stewardship in the time we have left. Our dedication to the stewardship that God has commanded us to exercise is reflected in the manner in which we administer and care for our possessions. We have to keep in mind that God Himself has given us custody of these resources, and we are responsible for properly managing them in light of that fact.

In Colossians 3:23-24, the Apostle Paul gives us the following admonition: "Whatever you do, work at it with all your heart, as working for the Lord, not for human masters, since you know that you will receive an inheritance from the Lord as a reward. " You are not serving yourself but rather the Lord Jesus Christ." This text reminds us that when we are getting our property ready for sale, we should work with the same level of attention and honesty as if we were serving Christ Himself. It is not enough for us to just maximize our profits; the caliber of the job we produce must also bring glory to God.

In his book "God Is at Work: Transforming People and Nations Through Business," the well-known Christian businessman and author Ken Eldred writes that "Christian businesspeople possess an incredible opportunity to impact the Kingdom through what they do best: business." They are considered to be in the "front lines" of the growth of the Kingdom.

When approaching the process with this frame of mind, preparing a home for sale involves more than just cleaning and repairing the house; rather, it is making sure that each decision, each repair, and each enhancement honors God. Our objective is not simply to turn a profit; rather, we want to demonstrate that we have been responsible stewards of what God has given to us.

As we move on with this procedure, let us pledge to working in a conscientious and trustworthy manner. Let us approach this endeavor with a spirit of service, regarding each stage as a chance to bring glory to God in some way. Every duty is an opportunity for us to display our commitment to godly stewardship, whether it be picking the right contractors, investing in required improvements, or just cleaning and staging the property.

Marketing Your Property: Honesty and Integrity in Business

The process of marketing a piece of real estate is an art form that calls for careful planning and creative thought. However, as followers of Christ, our strategy for conducting business must also be deeply anchored in the principles of honesty and integrity. Our conduct in business should always be reflective of the Christian ideals that we hold in high regard.

The words of Proverbs 10:9 provide us some words of encouragement when they state, "Whoever walks in integrity walks securely," yet the verse also says that "whoever takes crooked paths will be found out." This passage serves as a reminder to portray our property in an honest and ethical manner when selling it, which is the context in which it is found. It is quite simple to slip into the trap of emphasizing the property's features or glossing over its flaws; but, as followers of Christ, it is imperative that we avoid falling into these traps. In his book "There's No Such Thing as Business Ethics," best-selling Christian author and successful businessman John C. Maxwell wrote, "There's no such thing as business ethics. When it comes to making choices, there is only one rule to follow: the Golden Rule. Let's keep this Golden Rule in mind as we go about marketing our homes and do our best to treat prospective purchasers the way that we would want to be treated ourselves.

As a result, we will maintain the highest levels of honesty and integrity throughout the process of determining the price, writing property descriptions, and interacting with prospective purchasers. We shall not make any remarks or use any photographs that could be construed as deceptive. Instead, we will focus on highlighting the genuine worth and potential of the property. Not only do we want to make sure that we have a successful sale of our homes, but we also want to honor God and be a witness to our religion, therefore we have decided to market them in this manner.

In this part of the discussion, we'll look at some practical marketing methods while always making sure to ground them in these Biblical principles. Our objective is not simply to close a deal on a piece of real estate; rather, we want to demonstrate an approach to doing business that is a testament to the fidelity and honesty of the children of God.

Negotiating a Sale: Conducting Business with Christian Values

When selling a home, one of the most important steps in the process is to enter into talks with the potential buyer. In this time, not only does strategic acumen but also emotional intelligence need to be utilized. As followers of Christ, it is also our responsibility to ensure that the way we conduct business is consistent with Christian principles, as this will serve as a demonstration of our faith.

A reminder of this can be found in Philippians 2:3, which states, "Do nothing out of selfish ambition or pretentious conceit. Instead, humble yourself and value others more than you value yourself. This profound passage of scripture encourages us to go into negotiations not simply with the intention of maximizing our own profits, but also with a mindset that places a high value on fairness and respects the opposing party.

Mike Murdock, a prominent Christian author, wrote an influential book titled "The Businessman's Topical Bible," in which he asserts that "Negotiation is simply communication with results." However, as Christian investors, we are aware that'results' encompass more than just the final selling price of an asset. In addition to this, they include the honesty and fairness that we uphold during the entire procedure, as well as the testimony that we provide.

As we proceed through this part, we will discuss numerous approaches and strategies for negotiating. But more than that, we will discuss how to use these tools in a way that gives priority to fairness, respects the dignity of all persons involved, and is consistent with our Christian faith. When we do this, we establish transactions that are respectful to God and that reflect the values of love and fairness that He upholds.

Mental State: Detaching Emotions from Selling: A Lesson in Non-Attachment

In selling an investment property, it's not uncommon for emotions to run high. This can be especially true if the property has been in your possession for a long time, or if it holds special significance. Yet, as investors, and more so as Christians, we are called to approach this phase with a sense of non-attachment.

A reminder of this can be found in Philippians 2:3, which states, "Do nothing out of selfish ambition or pretentious conceit. Instead, humble yourself and value others more than you value yourself. This profound passage of scripture encourages us to go into negotiations not simply with the intention of maximizing our own profits, but also with a mindset that places a high value on fairness and respects the opposing party.

Mike Murdock, a prominent Christian author, wrote an influential book titled "The Businessman's Topical Bible," in which he asserts that "Negotiation is simply communication with results." However, as Christian investors, we are aware that'results' encompass more than just the final selling price of an asset. In addition to this, they include the honesty and fairness that we uphold during the entire procedure, as well as the testimony that we provide.

As we proceed through this part, we will discuss numerous approaches and strategies for negotiating. But more than that, we will discuss how to use these tools in a way that gives priority to fairness, respects the dignity of all persons involved, and is consistent with our Christian faith. When we do this, we establish transactions that are respectful to God and that reflect the values of love and fairness that He upholds.

This enlightening journey through the process of selling investment properties, has imparted a wealth of biblical wisdom. Each phase – discerning when and why to sell, preparing the property for sale, marketing, negotiating, and managing our emotions – showcases how our Christian faith offers valuable guidance.

The aim of this section was to interweave practical real estate knowledge with biblical principles, reminding us that God's wisdom and guidance are paramount in every business undertaking. From discerning the right timing according to Ecclesiastes 3:1, striving for excellent stewardship as per Colossians 3:23, to maintaining honesty and integrity based on Proverbs 10:9, our faith enriches our approach to selling properties.

Indeed, a heart at peace, as Proverbs 14:30 encourages, isn't merely beneficial for our emotional well-being; it also allows us to conduct our real estate transactions with grace and wisdom. As we navigate the complex world of real estate, may we continue to incorporate these lessons into our practices, reflecting Christ in our business dealings and honoring God through our investments.

Rental Properties and Landlording

Why Rental Properties? Serving Others Through Providing Shelter:

The accumulation of wealth can be accomplished in a variety of ways, one of which is through investing in rental homes. It affords us the chance to put our faith into action and heed the call we have received to serve the needs of others. This viewpoint, which views service in the form of investment as a type of service, is consistent with a central principle of the Christian faith, which is the mandate to love and serve our neighbors.

In essence, rental properties give us the opportunity to fulfill one of the most essential requirements of existence, which is the need for shelter. This is not a contribution of insignificant importance. To the contrary, it has a profound resonance with the command that Christ gave to us in Matthew 20:28. In that passage, He emphasizes His purpose, which is "not to be served, but to serve, and to give his life as a ransom for many." We are contributing to a larger divine purpose to serve humanity by fulfilling the need for housing that is not only secure, but also of high quality and reasonable cost.

This idea has been articulated in a way that is consistent with the teachings of prominent Christian financial counselors. The key publication "Business by the Book," written by Larry Burkett, makes the claim that "God entrusts us with His money not to build our own kingdom but to build His." The essential proposition of this argument is that all of our business and investment activities, including those related to real estate, should eventually be directed toward the fulfillment of a goal that is loftier than the simple accumulation of wealth.

In his book "Your Money Counts," the prolific author on Christian finance and co-founder of Crown Financial Ministries Howard Dayton further underlines this point by writing, "When we accepted Christ into our life, we became God's stewards.

We made the decision to deliberately give up control of our lives as well as our finances and give them over to God. When we apply this knowledge to our experiences thus far as real estate investors, we have realized that owning and overseeing rental properties is more than just a series of financial transactions. This presents a chance to love and serve others in the manner of Christ. We are not simply carrying out a business process when we perform normal maintenance or get a home ready for rent; rather, we are doing both of these things simultaneously. Instead, we are actively engaging in a divine plan by making use of the resources that have been entrusted to us in order to make a difference for the better in the lives of others.

Let us keep this greater calling in mind as we work our way through the complexities of managing rental properties and owning investment real estate in the next parts. The adoption of this perspective has the potential to infuse our investment journey with a sense of purpose that not only bolsters our financial efforts but also increases the depth of our faith and has an effect on the lives of those we serve.

Finding and Managing Tenants: Love Your Neighbor as Yourself

When it comes to the world of real estate investment, the task of locating and managing tenants becomes an important part of our path. These jobs come with their own unique set of hurdles, which range from the logistical difficulties of locating renters who can be relied on to the difficulties of resolving any conflicts or other problems that may crop up during the lease. The deep mandate that "Love your neighbor as yourself," which is found in Mark 12:31, serves as a compass for us as Christians and directs how we address these issues.

This biblical precept guides our interactions with our renters, which go much beyond the requirements outlined in our lease, and it is this relationship that we value the most. It affords us the chance to demonstrate the love of Christ by the way we interact with those people in our lives. When we are screening new tenants, we make it a point to treat each individual with dignity and fairness from the very beginning, eliminating any kind of discrimination or bias. As stated in Matthew 7:12, we follow the golden rule and treat others the way we would like to be treated ourselves. Therefore, in everything, treat other people the way you would want them to treat you.

Interacting with tenants is about more than simply doing business; it is an opportunity to display the love of Christ in a way that is both tangible and applicable to everyday life. We want to demonstrate kindness, understanding, and patience in all that we do, whether it be addressing maintenance issues, negotiating rent, or settling conflicts. These are all virtues that Christ exemplifies, and we want to reflect that.

Ken McElroy, author of "The ABCs of Real Estate Investing," places a strong emphasis on the need of developing and sustaining positive connections with occupants of rental properties. This piece of advice is more than just a strategic option for Christians; rather, it is a straightforward application of the tenets of our faith. As Christians, we are commanded to love and respect all people, and as landlords, we are to offer this love to the people who rent from us.

Gary Keller, in his book "The Millionaire Real Estate Investor," emphasizes the need of maintaining a strong connection between a landlord and a tenant. He makes the observation that a successful real estate investor does not only invest in homes, but also in individuals. As investors who are also Christians, we feel a strong connection to this point of view. We are aware that our renters are not only a potential source of money but also members of our community who are deserving of our love, respect, and thoughtfulness.

We are reminded of the love commandment as we go more into the practicalities of tenant management, and we make it a point to try to demonstrate love in each and every interaction. Our goal is to not only be landlords, but also neighbors, modeling the love of Christ in all of our interactions and turning the process of investing into a channel through which we can serve others and conduct mission.

Managing Rental Properties: Stewardship in Practice:

The management of rental properties is not only a financial venture, but also a spiritual exercise in the practice of good stewardship. This is because the management of rental properties requires good stewardship. The principle of stewardship is highlighted repeatedly throughout the Bible, and it serves as the foundation for our mentality when it comes to our financial holdings. According to what is written in 1 Peter 4:10, "Each of you should use whatever gift you have received to serve others, as faithful stewards of God's grace in its various forms."

Our rental properties are, in a very real sense, gifts from God that he has given to us. As a result, it is our duty to oversee their management with the highest levels of care, caution, and honesty. In this sense, stewardship involves more than simply ensuring that the property is well maintained. It entails making the most of the value and potential of the property in a way that is beneficial to our tenants and serves our communities, all while staying in accordance with the principles that we hold dear according to our faith.

Dave Ramsey stresses the significance of prudently managing our resources throughout "The Total Money Makeover," which may be found on his website. When we look at things from a Christian worldview, we recognize that our homes, cars, and other assets do not legally belong to us; rather, we are merely the stewards of what God has bestowed upon us. Our strategy for the administration of our rental properties will need to be revised in light of this new understanding.

Rob Kuban, in his book "The Christian's Guide to Financial Freedom," places a strong emphasis on the stewardship principle found throughout the Bible. He makes the point that taking care of God's property in a manner that is respectful to Him is not only a responsibility; it is also a pleasure that can provide one happiness and a sense of accomplishment. Because of this stewardship mindset, we make it a point to check on the comfort and security of our rental properties on a regular basis to ensure that they meet the needs of our tenants. In addition, we make it a priority to foster a feeling of community and belonging among individuals who call one of our locations home. In doing so, we acknowledge the fact that we are giving more than just a place to sleep; rather, we are making a contribution to the way people's lives and communities are woven together.

As we go more into the subject of property management, we are going to discuss several useful tactics and pointers, with the overarching concept of stewardship serving as our guiding light throughout. There is an opportunity for us to be good stewards of God's blessings in every circumstance we find ourselves in, in every choice we make, in every conversation we have with tenants or contractors, and in every action we do. By taking this approach, our role is elevated from that of simple landlords to that of ambassadors of God's grace. As a result, our real estate investments are transformed into platforms on which we can do service and minister to others.

Dealing with Common Landlord Issues: Conflict Resolution in the Bible:

We can expect to face a variety of difficulties associated with being a landlord in any project involving property management that we undertake. These may include rent payments that are late, property damage, violations of the lease, or disagreements amongst tenants. The Bible provides Christians with a road map to follow while navigating difficult situations, despite the fact that the problems themselves may seem overwhelming.

The Bible offers us universally applicable guidelines that we can put into practice when dealing with circumstances like these. The verses found in Matthew 18:15-17 are an indispensable resource for settling disagreements. It says, "If your brother or sister sins, go and point out their fault between the two of you, just as between two brothers and sisters." You have successfully won them over if they are listening to what you have to say. But if they refuse to listen, bring along one or two more people with you so that 'any subject may be established by the evidence of two or three witnesses.' If they continue to refuse to listen, you should alert the church; and if they refuse to listen even to the church, you should handle them the same way you would a pagan or a tax collector. This teaches us numerous important lessons, including the importance of direct communication, escalation only when absolutely required, and making resolution and reconciliation our primary goals at all times. In the context of managing rental properties, this can mean having a conversation about the problem with the renter who is directly affected by it, going to mediation if the early attempts to settle the problem do not succeed, and only contemplating eviction or legal action as a last resort.

On the other hand, our strategy for resolving conflicts does not simply consist of putting in place a mechanism; rather, it emphasizes cultivating the appropriate mentality and point of view. In his book titled "The Peacemaker," Ken Sande outlines an effective strategy for resolving conflicts according to the Bible. He places a strong emphasis on the significance of working for peace, disregarding infractions of a small kind, and seeking reconciliation with a spirit of humility and love.

The direction that Sande provides enlightens us to the fact that the resolution of conflicts is not only about finding a solution to a problem; rather, it is about glorifying God in how we interact with others, including our tenants. We demonstrate the love of Christ and cultivate relationships that are based on mutual understanding and respect when, despite our differences with one another, we treat others with kindness, compassion, and respect.

As we go further into the widespread problems that landlords face, we will investigate the sound guidance offered by seasoned real estate specialists and, along the process, we will use the Bible as our guide. As Christians, one of our primary goals should be to resolve disagreements in a way that honors God and communicates the depth of His love to others.

Mental State: Being a Successful Landlord from a Christian Perspective:

The job of a landlord can be emotionally taxing because it involves a variety of obligations, including interacting with tenants, managing properties, and ensuring that the investments will continue to be profitable. These obstacles might, at times, feel insurmountable, which can contribute to feelings of tension and anxiety. However, as Christians, we have a distinct viewpoint that might assist us in navigating the issues that we face. Because of our faith, we are able to keep a sound mental condition, which in turn enables us to provide excellent service to our renters and to manage our properties in an effective manner.

The letter that Paul wrote to the Philippians has a soothing promise that might serve as a compass for us as we navigate the challenges of property management. In the book of Philippians chapter 4, verse 7, it is said that "And the peace of God, which surpasses all understanding, will guard your hearts and your minds in Christ Jesus." This passage of scripture exhorts us to rely on the peace that only God can give to protect our mental health, a calm that is beyond our ability to understand. When we put our faith in the things that God has promised, we are able to discover a peace that is unshakeable, even in the midst of the chaos that being a landlord might at times bring.

This serenity does not come from passivity or complacency; rather, it enables us to be active stewards of our properties without feeling overburdened by the obligations that come with that role. It gives us the mental strength to make sound judgments, respond effectively to disputes, and serve our renters with service of the highest possible caliber.

In addition, if you are a Christian landlord, you should strive to have a spirit of service, which is a reflection of the life of servitude that Christ led. This perspective might help us see difficulties not simply as impediments, but as chances to demonstrate God's love to our residents and advance in our own spiritual walk, rather than as stumbling blocks.

The obligations of being a landlord require us to have knowledge and judgment so that we can successfully balance those demands with our personal life. Scripture implores us to strive for equilibrium in all aspects of our lives. In Ecclesiastes chapter 3, verse 1, it is written that "there is a time for everything, and a season for every activity under the heavens." This biblical passage can serve as a map for us to follow as we seek to strike a balance between our responsibilities as landlords, our personal life, and our spiritual development.

In this part of the discussion, we will investigate various methods that can help us have a positive mental attitude and strike a balance between the responsibilities we have as landlords and the other aspects of our lives. Throughout this entire process, we will be reminded that our ultimate strength and peace derive from the fact that we rely on God. Not only do we want to be the best property managers we can be, but we also want to honor God in everything that we do as successful Christians in the real estate industry.

In this examination of rental properties and the business of renting them out, we have combined principles of the Christian faith with many practical solutions. As we've seen, answering Christ's call to serve others by offering a roof over their heads in the form of rental properties is one way to directly put that calling into action. Interactions and relationships with renters offer an invaluable chance to put the golden rule, which states that we should love our neighbors as much as we love ourselves, into reality.

We studied the importance that the Bible places on stewardship, and we tried to model that importance in the way that we managed and took care of our assets. Biblical wisdom provides a framework for conflict resolution, enabling open dialogue, understanding, and forgiveness when inevitable disagreements emerge.

When discussing the mental challenges that come with being a landlord, we emphasized the significance of our faith in providing both mental and emotional strength, which helps us maintain a healthy balance between the various demands of property management and personal life. Let's make sure that, as we move forward, we continue to align our journey in landlording with the teachings of our faith, seeking not just financial gain but also spiritual growth and service to others in our quest to become better landlords.

Real Estate Flipping

Understanding Property Flipping: Capitalizing on Opportunities

The world of real estate investing is far more than a mere commercial effort; it is a setting in which we can actively put our faith into action and demonstrate its power. Every interaction provides us with the chance to live out our

Christian principles by behaving with honesty, compassion, and a sense of responsibility. This is stressed in Colossians 3:23-24: "Whatever you do, work at it with all your heart, as working for the Lord, not for human masters, since you know that you will receive an inheritance from the Lord as a reward. Work for the Lord, not for human masters." You are not serving yourself but rather the Lord Jesus Christ." Our goal in the business of flipping houses is not just to make a profit; rather, we want to serve the Lord with the labor of our hands and reflect His nature in the way we conduct ourselves in the marketplace.

Furthermore, flipping real estate provides a platform to display effective stewardship of the wealth that God has provided to us. This is a significant benefit. We buy properties that are either undervalued or in need of care, put in the time, effort, and financial investment to improve them, and then sell them to new owners so that they may continue to profit from the improvements we made. In a sense, we are serving as guardians of these properties, increasing the value of each one while also having a positive effect on the surrounding neighborhood.

However, there are several obstacles to overcome when flipping real estate. There is the potential for loss, and the path to profitable selling can sometimes be a difficult one, laden as it is with challenges and obstacles that were not anticipated. Despite this, we are not deterred by the difficulties. Instead, we look at them as a necessary step on the path that molds and builds our character as we travel it. According to Romans 5:3-5, which is quoted above, "...we also glory in our sufferings," because we are aware that suffering generates perseverance; perseverance produces character; and character produces hope. And hope doesn't make us look foolish because the love of God has been poured out into our hearts by the Holy Spirit, who has been given to us. Therefore, learning how to navigate the hurdles of property flipping becomes a great exercise in character development. We nurture endurance, develop resilience, and grow in faith as we face and overcome each hurdle that stands in our way. We get direct experience of the reality of Romans 8:28, which states, "And we know that in all things God works for the good of those who love him, who have been called according to his purpose." During this process, we have direct experience of the truth of this verse. We are able to transform the problems and risks that are connected with property flipping into opportunities for progress, both financially and spiritually, if we seek the guidance and wisdom of God.

In addition to this, buying and selling real estate is a tangible means to demonstrate the transformative power of God. We are also in the process of transforming properties, just like God is in the business of transforming people's lives. Just as God takes our lives, which have been tainted by sin and mistakes, and transforms us into new creations through the power of His love and grace, we take homes that have been abandoned or undervalued and give them a new lease on life. To summarize, flipping real estate presents an opportunity to not only create wealth but also, and perhaps more importantly, to demonstrate God's beliefs in the business world. This demonstrates that the Word of God is relevant and helpful in all aspects of life, including the business of real estate investing, which is a testimony to the truth that we are bearing by doing this. As a result, the way in which we invest in real estate becomes an act of worship and service. This exemplifies our determination to connect every part of our lives, including the work that we do for a living, with the teachings of the Bible and the plans that God has for the universe.

Finding Flip-Worthy Properties: Seeking God's Guidance

In the search for homes that are suitable for flipping, our attention is focused on more than just sound business practices. We want to cultivate a mutually beneficial link between our spiritual beliefs and the work that we do professionally, so we are working to integrate the two. We try to put the words of Colossians 3:17, which says "And whatever you do, whether in word or deed, do it all in the name of the Lord Jesus, giving thanks to God the Father through him," into practice in every aspect of our lives, including the business of buying and selling real estate. Finding undervalued properties that have room for improvement and expansion is an important part of our journey. This undertaking is not at all undertaken solo. As followers of Christianity, we put our faith in the guidance and understanding offered by an all-knowing God. It is important to remember the words of Proverbs 3:5-6, which say, "Trust in the LORD with all your heart, and do not lean on your own understanding; in all your ways submit to him, and he will make your paths straight." During our hunt for homes that are suitable for flipping, this passage encourages us to draw on the immense wisdom that God possesses.

During this process, the guidance of God may present itself in a variety of different ways. It could take the form of a subtle nudge in the direction of a property that others have overlooked, the capacity to identify promise in a home that has fallen into disrepair, or an instinctive avoidance of a deal that appears profitable but is high risk. We continue to keep an open mind and be receptive to these divine hints, as we are aware that they frequently determine the difference between a profitable flip and an unsuccessful one.

While we put our trust in God's insight, we also recognize that it is our job to conduct thorough research. This requires conducting exhaustive research, seeking the assistance of qualified professionals where appropriate, and maintaining a thorough approach throughout the whole property hunt. According to the wisdom found in Proverbs 14:15, "The simple believe anything, but the prudent give thought to their steps." When we are looking for properties, we incorporate both spiritual guidance and practical procedures into our search. Extensive market research, property valuation, and analysis of neighborhood trends are all activities that we partake in. While all this is going on, we are always seeking God's direction through prayer, introspection, and careful consideration. We recognize that our comprehension and information are restricted, and we humbly submit ourselves to the superior wisdom of God.

When it comes down to it, looking for houses to flip involves more than just the possibility of making a profit. It is a journey of the spirit that compels us to put into practice the doctrine found in Philippians 2:13, which states that "for it is God who works in you to will and to act in order to fulfill his good purpose." Our dependence on God is strengthened along with our relationship with Him as a result of this journey, and we are inspired to pursue our financial goals in a way that brings glory to Him while we do so. By incorporating prayer into our search process, we encourage God to direct us to the properties that contain promise for flipping, and we get closer to Him, which in turn strengthens our trust in and reliance on Him.

Managing Renovations: Demonstrating Good Stewardship

Once a home that is ideal for flipping has been located and acquired, the next critical step is the management of the modifications that will be done to the property. At this point in the process, you will need to pay minute attention to every detail, be able to manage resources efficiently, and make solid decisions. In its most basic form, overseeing restorations is a concrete demonstration of stewardship, a concept that is profoundly ingrained in the teachings of Christianity. According to the verse 1 Peter 4:10 in the Bible, we are instructed to "Each of you should use whatever gift you have received to serve others, as faithful stewards of God's grace in its various forms." In the context of the business of buying and selling real estate, this verse encourages us to make responsible and effective use of our skills, abilities, and resources during the phase of property renovation.

In this situation, practicing good stewardship requires exercising sound judgment when determining whether improvements will result in a material increase in the value of the property. It include managing the budget effectively in order to avoid excessive expenditures, ensuring that the work that is being done is of a good quality, and treating everyone who is participating in the renovation process with equity and decency. We are obligated to maintain a spirit of excellence because we are aware that the work that we do serves a more important purpose.

In addition, managing renovations involves more than just the physical refurbishing of the space; it also involves managing the human resources in an elegant and dignified manner. It entails making sure that everyone who is working on the project is treated with dignity and consideration, in accordance with the central tenet of Christianity, which is to "love your neighbor as yourself" (Mark 12:31). In addition to this, it entails effectively managing one's time as well as one's money resources in order to prevent squandering them, which is a reflection of the idea outlined in the parable of the talents (Matthew 25:14-30).

We regard the phase of renovation not only as a way to increase the value of a house but also as a platform to enact Christian ideals of fairness, respect, and love. This is how we approach the process. It is a chance to put into practice the advice given in Colossians 3:23, which says, "Whatever you do, work at it with all your heart, as working for the Lord, and not for human masters."

Our Christian beliefs serve as a compass to help us navigate the complexities of renovation management, and we make it a point to ensure that our actions reflect the accountability we have as stewards of God's property. When we tackle the process of transforming a home via renovations, we do so with a heart and mind that are focused on service and excellence, and we reflect our Christian faith in every decision and action that we make. As a result, the management of restorations transforms into a spiritual activity that demonstrates responsible stewardship.

Selling and Profiting: Ethical Considerations from a Biblical Perspective

Selling the property once it has been remodeled and making a return off of the investment represents the pinnacle of the process of flipping houses. The Christian religion that we practice tells us, on the other hand, that this is not only about monetary gain; rather, it is also about considering and supporting ethical standards that are consistent with the teachings of the Bible. According to 1 Timothy chapter six verse ten, which is quoted above, "For the love of money is a root of all kinds of evil." In their pursuit of wealth, several individuals have strayed from the true faith and caused themselves untold suffering as a result.

When it comes to the sale of the property, it is of the utmost significance that we conduct ourselves in a manner that is honest, fair, and honorable. We have a responsibility to make certain that all of the enhancements and renovations have been completed in accordance with the applicable codes and that prospective purchasers are provided with comprehensive information regarding the state of the property. Any flaws or shortcomings shouldn't be concealed or misrepresented, especially in light of Proverbs 11:3, which reads, "The integrity of the upright guides them, but the unfaithful are destroyed by their duplicity."

Another essential factor to take into account is the property's just asking price. To make an excessive profit, we must not take advantage of the current state of the market or the ignorance of our customers. An ethical approach to pricing is one that is consistent with the biblical teaching found in Leviticus 25:14, which states, "If you sell land to any of your own people or buy land from them, do not take advantage of each other."

It is imperative that, in the event that a profit is eventually made, we recognise that it is God's providence that paves the way for us to accumulate money (Deuteronomy 8:18). As a consequence of this, the distribution and application of our profits ought to be a reflection of both our devotion to God and our desire to be of service to others. This may take the form of donating to charitable organizations, reinvesting in the local community, or setting aside a percentage of our profits as a tithe.

Selling investment property and making a profit from the transaction both present chances for us to live out our Christian ideals and put them into practice. It gives one the opportunity to demonstrate to other people that managing one's business in a manner that is honoring to God is not only possible but also rewarding. This may be a precarious balancing act that requires careful navigation, but if we take an approach that is characterized by prayer and reflection, we can be successful while being true to our Christian ideals. In this sense, the act of flipping real estate becomes not only a lucrative business effort but also an expression of our faith and dedication to Godly principles. In other words, it goes beyond simply being a lucrative economic endeavor.

Mental State: The Risks and Rewards of Flipping

The business of flipping houses, despite the fact that it can result in considerable profits if successful, is not without its share of inherent dangers. Having a healthy mental state that is robust is necessary in order to effectively manage these uncertainties. Within the framework of our Christian faith, we find strength and encouragement in the scriptural verse that may be found in Joshua 1:9, which reads, "Have I not commanded you? Maintain your fortitude and bravery. Do not be afraid, and do not let discouragement get the better of you, because the Lord your God will be with you wherever you go. This heavenly guarantee strengthens us, which enables us to remain unwavering and resilient in the face of the challenges and difficulties that are inherent in the business of flipping houses.

The process of flipping real estate can elicit a tornado of feelings, from the excitement that comes with the prospect of finding a prospective flip to the stress that comes with supervising repairs and the anxiety that comes with selling the home. These contrasting states of emotion have the potential to put a significant strain on our mental health, highlighting the need of cultivating a state of mind that is characterized by calmness and unshakeable confidence in the supreme authority that God has.

Furthermore, the inherent dangers, such as unanticipated renovation costs, unplanned shifts in the real estate market, or difficulties in selling the home, can give rise to feelings of concern and tension. Nevertheless, we are able to battle these unfavorable feelings if we rely on our faith and remember the promises that God has given us. Philippians 4:6-7 contains a reminder of this fact: "Do not be worried about anything; rather, in everything, submit your requests to God via prayer and supplication, together with thanksgiving. And the peace of God, which surpasses all comprehension, will protect your hearts and your minds in the name of Jesus Christ.

For a successful journey through the challenges and opportunities presented by property flipping, it is essential to keep a strong mental state. Our religious beliefs not only instruct us in the appropriate manner in which to conduct our commercial activities, but they also give us with the spiritual resources that enable us to maintain our emotional and mental equilibrium amidst the ups and downs that are an inevitable part of the process of flipping houses. Through the adoption of this well-rounded strategy, we are able to transform the act of flipping real estate into something much more than an economic venture; it becomes an opportunity for spiritual growth and fortitude, as well as an expression of our trust in and dependence on the guidance and provision of God.

As we draw to a close on our examination of flipping houses from a Christian point of view, it is essential that we pause to consider the ways in which our pursuit of professional success is intertwined with our maturation as spiritual beings. As we've seen, every stage of the house-flipping process presents us with a chance to put our faith into practice, show that we're excellent stewards of our resources, and show that we behave honestly and with integrity. This includes selecting houses that are suitable for flipping, managing improvements, and selling the property for a profit.

However, perhaps the most important thing that we've realized is that flipping houses can be a wonderful exercise in trusting and depending on God, particularly when it comes to overcoming the mental and emotional problems that come along with it. We are reminded of passages such as Philippians 4:6-7, which encourage us not to be anxious but, rather, to present our prayers to God, confident in the certainty that His peace will guard both our hearts and minds.

When it comes down to it, the journey of flipping houses is about more than simply the possible cash rewards. It is about setting out on an adventure that forces us to mature, to rely on the understanding that God provides, and to strengthen our faith. This is evidence that the promise that God made in Romans 8:28 will be fulfilled: "And we know that in all things God works for the good of those who love him, who have been called according to his purpose," the Bible says. "Also, we know that the Holy Spirit will guide us into all truth." It is about making the most of our abilities, gifts, and opportunities so that we might bring honor to God and serve a higher purpose. We are not merely trading real estate; rather, we are developing and cultivating our connection with God while making constructive contributions to the communities in which we live. That is the real benefit of investing in real estate flips.

Tax Benefits and Implications

Understanding Real Estate Taxation: Render unto Caesar

It is essential that we keep in mind the biblical teaching that instructs us to "Render unto Caesar the things that are Caesar's, and unto God the things that are God's." as we pursue the business of flipping real estate. According to what

Jesus says in Mark 12:17, the principle instructs us to revere and adhere by the regulations and laws of our land, which in our situation includes tax laws. We should do this because it is right.

The taxation aspect of the business of flipping houses is not something that can be ignored, despite the fact that it may appear to be overwhelming. Because of the intricate nature of the taxation rules related with property flipping, it is imperative that we have a comprehensive understanding of the relevant legislation in order to ensure that our business practices are compliant with the relevant laws. On the one hand, it is our duty to fulfill our tax responsibilities, and on the other, we have the ability to make the most of the tax benefits that are legally and morally permissible for us to take advantage of. Understanding the distinction between income tax and the capital gains tax is essential for getting a handle on real estate taxation since these two types of taxes are utilized in very different ways within the real estate industry. Generally speaking, the capital gains tax is applicable to real estate investments made for a longer period of time, but the income tax is more pertinent for investments made for a shorter period of time, such as property flipping, which is typically considered to be a company.

While we are working hard to understand and navigate the complexities of real estate taxation, we are also working hard to strengthen our devotion to godly principles by running our business in a way that demonstrates ethical behavior, respects the law, and ultimately praises God.

Common Deductions and Credits: Being Wise as Serpents

When flipping real estate, it can be intimidating to navigate the complex landscape of tax deductions and credits, but doing so is an essential component of effectively managing your company's financial obligations. As disciples of Christ, we are directed by the words of Matthew 10:16, which urge us to be "as shrewd as snakes and as innocent as doves." This shrewdness entails the intelligence to navigate our financial duties in a prudent and moral manner, making use of legitimate tax deductions and credits that could reduce our overall tax liability.

When it comes to the business of flipping houses, there are a number of standard deductions that we may take advantage of. These can include the interest on loans obtained for the purpose of purchasing or remodeling the property, the expenditures associated with repairs and maintenance, property taxes, insurance premiums, and even the expenses involved in promoting the property in preparation for its potential sale. In addition, there is a possibility that we will be eligible for some tax credits, such as the Rehabilitation Tax Credit, which offers financial incentives to encourage the preservation and rehabilitation of historic structures.

On the other hand, due to the intricacy and complexity of the tax regulations, it is absolutely necessary to seek the assistance of a tax professional. They are able to provide us with assistance in accurately identifying all of the available deductions and credits, so guaranteeing that we do not overlook any potential advantages by accident. This is in keeping with the biblical mandate that we should be wise stewards of the resources God has given us, carefully managing our finances within the bounds of law and the highest standards of morality.

We honor God by running our business in this manner, which demonstrates that our business practices are in line with the values that we defend as followers of Christ. In addition to achieving success in the real estate flipping business, one of our primary goals is to serve as a model of Christian morality in the commercial world, demonstrating that one's faith and one's professional life are not incompatible.

Tax Strategies for Real Estate Investors: Stewardship and Legality

Real estate investment and the business of flipping properties both require a solid understanding of the applicable tax laws and regulations. It entails having an awareness of the many tax rules and regulations, as well as coming up with plans to minimize tax responsibilities while still adhering to the parameters set by the law. In light of the fact that we are responsible stewards of the resources that God has entrusted to us, our attitude to the management of our tax obligations ought to reflect wisdom and prudence.

Real estate investors have access to a wide variety of tax planning options that they can take advantage of. For instance, a 1031 exchange, so-called because it is named after Section 1031 of the Internal Revenue Code of the United States, enables investors to postpone the payment of capital gains tax by reinvesting the proceeds from the sale of a property in another property that is of the same sort. Alternately, converting a property that is being flipped into a rental could result in different tax benefits, such as the ability to deduct certain expenses linked to the property's maintenance and depreciation.

Nevertheless, it is absolutely necessary to implement these techniques in a way that is not just legal but also ethical. "Let everyone be subject to the governing authorities, for there is no authority except that which God has established," it says in Romans 13:1-2. God is the one who founded all of the existing powers and institutions. Consequently, everyone who rebels against the authority is also revolting against what God has established, and those who do so will bring punishment on themselves. This passage of scripture emphasizes the significance of abiding by tax rules as an integral component of our larger commitment to living in accordance with God's directives.

It is highly recommended that you get the advice of a tax expert or an attorney who specializes in real estate tax law before making any decisions on real estate investments due to the complicated nature of tax laws and the effects these laws have. These professionals can assist you in ensuring that you are not only efficiently lowering your tax payments but also carrying out your business activities within the bounds of the law. By doing so, you can be sure that you are running your company in a manner that is in accordance with the laws of the land as well as the rules of God, so exemplifying the principle of good stewardship in all aspects of your property flipping business.

It is important to keep in mind that a good tax plan is about more than just cutting current expenses; it also helps to preserve the credibility of your company, protects you from the possibility of falling into legal traps, and reaffirms your role as a responsible Christian entrepreneur who seeks to honor God in all that you do.

Mental State: Understanding the Importance of Tax Planning

The endeavor of gaining an understanding of the significance of tax planning in the process of flipping real estate is one that has a strong resonance with the Christian ideals of stewardship, integrity, and wisdom. As we continue to delve deeper into this complex topic, it is essential to remember that tax planning is not only a financial exercise, but rather a reflection of our larger obligation to manage God's blessings in a responsible and ethical manner. This is something that needs to be kept in mind as we move forward.

In the context of taxes, planning goes beyond merely complying with the law. It requires an in-depth consideration of how various tax legislation and provisions apply to an individual's specific circumstances, a comprehension of the available chances to minimize liabilities, and the making of strategic decisions that are aligned with both financial goals and ethical ideals. In addition to this, it requires staying current on the ever-shifting tax regulations and the effects these changes have for the many different real estate investment techniques.

The following is a more in-depth examination of the complexity of tax preparation, as well as an explanation of why this aspect of the mental game in property flipping is so important:

1. Obeying the Law The passage in Romans 13:1-2 instructs us to submit to the governing authorities, which includes abiding by the rules pertaining to taxes. In addition to being required by law, compliance with these laws is also a moral requirement, since it demonstrates our dedication to acting in an honest and honorable manner.

2. **Strategic Planning and Decision Making**: Making use of various tax methods such as 1031 exchanges, leveraging depreciation, or comprehending the implications of capital gains demands in-depth knowledge as well as forethought. To make good use of these tactics, one needs to have a sharp mind and act in a responsible manner at all times; otherwise, they can become dangerous tools.

3. Continual Education Because of the fluid nature of tax law, it is critical to update one's knowledge on a consistent basis. This necessitates making a commitment to ongoing learning,

acquiring a grasp of newly enacted legislation, and applying those requirements to your own circumstances.

4. **Moral Responsibility**: Our choices in regards to money should always be in line with the Christian principles that we uphold. Although it is good corporate practice to try to minimize tax payments, this should never serve as an excuse to engage in dishonest or unethical activities. In Proverbs 11:3, the following verse is emphasized: "The integrity of the upright guides them, but the unfaithful are destroyed by their duplicity."

5. Taking Advantage of Professional Guidance Considering the intricacy of tax preparation, it is frequently prudent to seek out the professional guidance of tax specialists who are acquainted with real estate investment. They are able to provide insights that are customized to particular circumstances, ensuring compliance with the law while also maximizing the potential for legitimate savings opportunities.

6. A **Prayerful Approach**: Prayer, in which we seek God's wisdom and assistance in navigating these difficult issues, can be an essential component in our approach to tax preparation. James 1:5 encourages us to pray to God for wisdom, and promises that if we do, He will give it to us in abundance.

7. From a holistic point of view, tax preparation in real estate investing is not an independent facet of the business but

rather intertwined with other aspects such as finance, property selection, remodeling strategy, and sales technique. It is essential to have an understanding of how these factors interact with one another and determine tax implications.

In a nutshell, the frame of mind that is necessary for successful tax preparation in the process of property flipping is diverse and has strong roots in Christian ethics. It involves adhering to the law, engaging in strategic thinking, continuing one's education, maintaining moral integrity, working in conjunction with experts, practicing prayerful discernment, and having an overall comprehension of the company. We assert our duty as faithful stewards by tackling this task with dedication, ethics, and reliance on the wisdom of God. In this way, we respect God via our business practices, and we make decisions that reflect His teachings. It's going to be a tough road, but it's going to be worth it in the end because it's going to show us how well we can handle complicated situations by having faith and using our brains.

The book Tax Benefits and Implications led us through a thorough grasp of real estate taxation within the context of property flipping. The whole thing was based on the core Christian values that ought to govern our decisions and actions.

We have discussed the judicious combination of knowledge and responsibility that is necessary to navigate common deductions and credits, we have highlighted the importance of conducting various tax tactics in an ethical manner, and we have acknowledged the significance of maintaining a healthy mental state. The teachings of the Bible have, throughout history, provided both intellectual and spiritual sustenance to those who have studied them.

We were able to realize that our monetary responsibilities are not only about meeting requirements; rather, they represent an opportunity for us to glorify God and demonstrate good stewardship by interweaving the teachings of the Bible with our legal obligations. The challenge posed by the junction of law, morality, strategy, and the divine knowledge that we, as Christian investors, are guided to pursue is brought to light by the fact that we have been charged with being as "Wise as Serpents" in our approach.

This path also highlights the necessity for continual learning, guidance from professionals, and faith that is able to withstand challenges. We are completely capable of navigating these intricacies thanks to the power that comes from God, and our faith will serve as the foundation for the decisions that we make.

In the course of our investigation into tax planning, not only have we increased our comprehension of the technical aspects, but we have also created a spiritual tapestry that represents our larger call to live our lives, including our business activities, in accordance with the word of God. This spiritual tapestry is a direct result of our investigation. Every time we turn the page, we are reminded to do what is right, love mercy, and walk humbly with God in all that we do. By doing so, we can turn even the most mundane activities into chances to bring glory to God.

Building Your Real Estate Portfolio

Creating a Real Estate Investment Plan: Seeking God's Guidance

Putting together a real estate portfolio is a substantial endeavor that calls for intelligence, insight, and careful planning. As followers of Christ, this attempt is not only a financial one; rather, it is a spiritual one in which we seek to match our objectives and activities with the will of God.

The significance of seeking the direction and wisdom of God via prayer and introspection is something that needs to be acknowledged before we can proceed down this road. It is only via His wisdom that we have any possibility of arriving at choices that are consistent with the principles that will last forever. By consulting texts such as Proverbs 16:3, which says, "Commit to the Lord whatever you do, and he will establish your plans," we can help maintain the planning process rooted in faith and open our hearts to the divine knowledge that is available to us.

When we devote ourselves to studying the Word of God, we unearth truths that serve as a foundation for our decisions regarding money. These guiding principles offer a road map for bringing our investment strategies into alignment with ideals that go beyond merely achieving monetary success. We are aware that investment is about more than just making a profit; it also serves a purpose. We are able to elevate our investing plan to the level of a divine mission by establishing goals and objectives that reflect the love and provision of God. In addition, making sure that our plans are founded spiritually as well as financially by surrounding ourselves with godly mentors and counselors guarantees that our plans will be successful. We are commanded to make investments in properties and communities that serve as a testament to the grace of God while also providing homes for families and revitalizing areas.

We have a strategy that has been formed through prayer, and now we are moving forward in faith, hoping that God will direct our actions. Our decisions should always reflect Christ's love and righteousness, and our integrity should serve as our guide in making those decisions. Even though the world may present us with opportunities to cut corners, we continue to follow the straight and narrow path, secure in God's will. By keeping our investing strategy fresh in our minds and praying over it frequently, we stay in step with the will of God. As the markets move and new opportunities present themselves, we regularly bring our ideas before God, asking for His guidance and trusting that He is in complete charge of the situation.

In conclusion, the process of developing a plan for investing in real estate presents us with an opportunity to put our faith into action. When we seek the direction of God, study His Word, align our goals with His plan, and live in faith and integrity, we embark on a journey that extends far beyond the pursuit of financial gain. Faith, hope, and love are the eternal currencies that serve as the standard by which we evaluate our achievements, not dollars and cents. We are not simply accumulating assets; rather, we are laying the groundwork for a legacy that will last for all of eternity. This profoundly spiritual exercise is a perfect dance between earthly intelligence and heavenly guidance. The real investment that we are making here is not in bricks and mortar, but rather in the eternal kingdom of God.

Diversifying Your Portfolio: The Parable of the Talents Revisited

Real estate investing provides us with the chance to put into practice the discernment and stewardship that God has bestowed upon us. One of the most essential components of astute financial management is diversification, which refers to a tactic that entails distributing our capital across a number of distinct investment opportunities. This strategy enables us to reduce the likelihood of negative outcomes and bring our heavenly goals closer in line with God's heavenly ideals.

A significant scriptural guidance for this idea can be found in Matthew 25:14-30, which tells the story of the Parable of the Talents. Jesus relates the narrative of a master who divides out talents (a monetary unit) among his servants in accordance with their respective levels of ability in this parable. Two of the servants choose to invest their money and end up doubling it, while the third servant hides his talent away because he is afraid of losing it. The instructor commends those who made intelligent investments and reprimands the student who did not put the resources provided to him to good use.

This fable is not just about financial matters; rather, it teaches lessons about responsibility, initiative, and being a good steward. It exhorts us to acknowledge the resources that God has given us and to put those resources to work in a way that is both wise and purposeful. We put the teaching of the parable into practice by ensuring that we don't put all of our "financial eggs" into one "basket" through the practice of diversifying our investments.

But how exactly does one go about diversifying their holdings in a real estate investing portfolio? It is possible that this will involve investing in a variety of real estate, including residential, commercial, and rental properties. It could imply looking into prospects in a number of different geographical regions or market niches. It is about developing a diversified investment strategy that not only represents our monetary objectives but also our dedication to the values that God teaches us.

The story of the Talents serves as a reminder to us that we are responsible stewards of the resources that have been entrusted to us. Our investments are not only monetary transactions; rather, they are a demonstration of our fidelity and obedience to the calling that God has placed on our lives. We are stewards of the gifts that God has given us, and the manner in which we invest indicates how well we comprehend His will and His ways.

In conclusion, diversification is more than just a good method for making investments; it is a spiritual value that has its roots in the knowledge found in the bible. It exhorts us to be good stewards of the resources that God has given us by being active, wise, and faithful with those resources. It's not only about making as much money as possible; it's also about pleasing God with the decisions and deeds we make. The management of our investment portfolio presents us with the chance to put the teachings of Christ into practice, and in doing so, we bear witness to the goodness and insight of God in each and every facet of our lives. Our faith in God's provision and our determination to abide by His word are both reflected in a concrete way in the diverse portfolio that we have created.

Protecting Your Investments: The Biblical Concept of Covering

Investing in real estate is a challenging and lucrative business that also offers a wealth of possibilities to display Christian principles. Investors can bring glory to God by being good stewards of their money through careful planning, diversification, protection, and compliance with applicable tax rules.

Developing a solid strategy that is founded in faith is a vital step to take before beginning the process of investing in real estate. Investors can align their aims with God's will and wisdom by praying, reflecting, and reviewing scriptures like Proverbs 16:3, which says, "Commit to the Lord whatever you do, and he will establish your plans." Investors can do this by seeking the guidance of God via prayer and reflection.

When it comes to investing, diversification is a strategy that can be used to reduce risk. Taking their cue from the parable of the talents found in Matthew 25:14-30, astute investors know better than to put all of their financial "eggs" in one basket. This strategy is reflective of the call made in the Bible to prudently invest and diversify one's resources, exercising stewardship in a manner that is congruent with the lessons of the tale.

The Bible repeatedly underscores the significance of being responsible stewards of the things that have been given to us. The biblical principle of covering and safeguarding the resources that God has provided can be echoed by investors through the purchase of insurance, the establishment of appropriate legal structures, and the implementation of risk management measures.

Understanding tax laws and developing a strategy to minimize obligations while remaining in compliance with tax regulations are two essential components of effective tax planning for property flipping. Different tactics, such as employing a 1031 exchange to delay the payment of capital gains tax, represent both responsible management and compliance with the law. Romans 13:1–2 teaches us to be submissive to governing authorities and to respect God by obeying the rules of the land, including tax

The proper planning of taxes demands mental toughness, the ability to think strategically, and alignment with God's purpose. With the comfort found in Philippians 4:13, "I can do all things through Christ who strengthens me," investors are able to handle the complexity of tax preparation and make use of the wisdom and resilience that God offers.

It is a path that encompasses planning, diversification, protection, and having a detailed understanding of tax regulations in order to build and protect a real estate portfolio in accordance with Christian beliefs. This journey is thorough. Rather than only being a kind of prudent financial management, it elevates real estate investing to the level of a spiritually meaningful enterprise that is consistent with Christian beliefs and values. By showing reverence for God through these investments, one can shed light on the enduring virtues of stewardship, prudence, and faith that are essential to reaching one's financial goals.

Putting money into real estate is more than just a business gamble; it is a duty to be good stewards of the resources that God has given us. As we embark on the adventure of accumulating a real estate portfolio, the first thing we do is pray to God for wisdom and direction. It is essential, prior to starting down this road, to develop a solid investing strategy that is in accordance with His will. The verse Proverbs 16:3 tells us to "Commit to the Lord whatever you do, and he will establish your plans." This verse is a good reminder for us. As we progress, diversity will become an increasingly important tactic. This is not just a clever strategy for making investments; rather, it is a call to invest the resources that have been entrusted to us in a loyal manner. Matthew 25:14–30 contains a parable that helps us understand why it's important to diversify our sources of income rather than putting all of our "eggs" in one financial "basket." By taking this approach, we are better able to put into practice the stewardship and wisdom that are included within this biblical instruction.

The Bible imparts knowledge to us not just about defense but also about the significance of guarding what has been bestowed upon us. Our efforts to secure investments are an echo of the biblical concept of protecting and honoring the resources that God has provided, and they can take the form of insurance policies, legal structures, or risk management strategies.

Managing our investments effectively requires that we do routine evaluations and make required modifications. We ensure that our investment portfolio is in line with both current market conditions and Christian ideals by using caution and discernment in our decision-making. According to the guidance provided by Proverbs 22:3, we gain the knowledge that "the prudent see danger and take refuge, but the simple keep going and pay the penalty."

Even the mental side of investing, such as being aware of and making preparations for one's responsibilities regarding taxes, has resonance with our beliefs. In spite of the fact that the challenges may appear to be insurmountable, we can take comfort in the words of Philippians 4:13 which read, "I can do all things through Christ who strengthens me." God gives us the ability to negotiate the difficulties of tax planning and other challenges by providing us with wisdom and the strength to do so.

Creating a portfolio of real estate and being responsible for its management is a profoundly spiritual experience. It is not just about making a profit; rather, it is about good stewardship, wisdom, protection, and prudence, as well as being in accordance with the will of God. As we negotiate the complexity of the market with God's help, this financial adventure will become a living monument to our faith.

In the end, it's not just about amassing wealth; it's about leaving behind a legacy that glorifies God and helps advance His kingdom. We don't travel this holy path by ourselves; rather, we travel it with God, putting our faith in His provision, wisdom, and ultimate purpose. We are not just investors in real estate; rather, we are investors in a divine plan that goes beyond merely accumulating wealth in this world and reflects our will to conduct our lives in accordance with values that have an enduring impact.

Mental State: Strategic Thinking and Long-term Planning in Line with God's Plan

Establishing and sustaining a portfolio is more than a commercial endeavor; it's a spiritual journey that requires strategic thinking, long-term planning, and a mental condition that is strongly anchored in religion. Real estate investment is a fascinating and often hard subject, and establishing and maintaining a portfolio is more than a business exercise. This journey requires of us alignment with God's everlasting purpose, which calls for more than just financial savvy on our part.

Jeremiah 29:11 is a verse that should act as a constant reminder and a source of encouragement. It says, "For I know the plans I have for you, declares the Lord, plans for welfare and not for evil, to give you a future and a hope." These words are more than just a source of solace; rather, they are a rallying cry for action. They urge us to approach the business of real estate investing with a more expansive perspective, one that goes beyond the pursuit of monetary gain alone.

A Contemplative Approach to the Planning Process

Long-term planning in real estate isn't just about buying houses, watching our investments grow in value, or ensuring a comfortable financial future for ourselves. The goal is to recognize and act in accordance with God's will for everyone of our lives. It is a journey that begins with careful contemplation of our goals and concludes with the awareness that our worldly achievements are part of a divine orchestration. This journey begins with prayerful consideration of our goals and finishes with this realization.

In the context of this discussion, strategic thinking is not limited to spreadsheets, patterns in the market, or investment algorithms. It encompasses our capacity for spiritual discernment as well as our unshakeable dedication to bringing our goals into line with God's purpose. Each decision about investments turns into a prayerful choice, to be directed by God's knowledge and brought into alignment with His plan.

The Role of Belief as the Governing Principle

Investing in real estate can be laden with a lot of unpredictability and danger. There are a lot of moving parts, and the stakes are rather high. On the other hand, because we are God's children, we have access to a source of wisdom and direction that is much more profound than the understanding of this world.

Our faith is not merely a supporting role on this adventure; rather, it plays a pivotal role at the center. It serves as both a compass and a guiding star for us, as well as a source of reassurance that, despite the storms and uncertainties we face, we are proceeding along the route that God has paved for us.

The formation of a real estate portfolio involves more than the simple accumulation of assets; rather, it is the establishment of a spiritual dynasty. It's not enough to have business sense; you also need a heart that's tuned in to hear what God has to say so you can make decisions that reflect both. It's not just about making money; it's about using your resources in a way that serves others, honors God, and brings glory to himself. This chapter has took us on a journey, and it wasn't only about how to invest our money; it was also about our spiritual development. Constructing a real estate portfolio is an endeavor that is intricate and multifaceted, full of chances, obstacles, and lessons to be learned.

Every step of this journey is informed and enriched by our faith, beginning with the preliminary stages of planning, which were directed by the knowledge of God, and continuing on through the complicated dance of diversification, protection, and strategic decision-making.

Our experience has taught us that our financial transactions are not the same thing as our investments; rather, they are a sacred trust and a stewardship that requires us to uphold a higher level of honesty, wisdom, and compassion.

We are not merely tasked with the role of investors, motivated by monetary gain and societal acclaim. We are commanded to be good stewards, to be directed by a divine plan, and to be fully dedicated to bringing honor to God in all that we undertake.

As we come to the end of this chapter, let us ponder the important truth that the success of our real estate investing endeavors, as well as our lives in general, is not evaluated in monetary terms but rather in the depth of our relationship with God.

This is a trip that requires not just a financial investment from us, but also an investment of our minds, hearts, and souls. It is a way that is replete with assurance, as it is led by a loving God who guarantees a future that is bright with possibility.

We are not on our own in the holy quest of accumulating and managing a portfolio of real estate investments. We are certain that God has a good and perfect plan for our life, and we walk hand in hand with him, safe in the knowledge that he is wise, provides for us, and loves us forever. It is a path that is full of grace, growth, and meaning for all of eternity.

The Investor Mindset

When considered from a Christian perspective, the act of investing is a deep test of one's faith, knowledge, and stewardship. Investing is commonly seen as a route to monetary gain, a method to get security, and even a game to win all over the world. Investing, on the other hand, is a spiritual journey for those who follow Christ, one that is aligned with the kingdom of God and the eternal principles that it upholds.

The Ownership Belongs to God, and We Are His Stewards

The first step in the path is gaining a profound comprehension that God is the owner of everything. According to the first verse of Psalm 24, which is often quoted, "the earth is the Lord's, and everything in it." Recognizing that God is the owner releases us from the responsibility of possessing and exercising control over our possessions. We, on the other hand, take on the role of stewards, managing the resources God has given us with honesty, knowledge, and a sense of purpose that goes beyond pursuing our own personal gain.

141

Our choices in regards to investments are not determined exclusively by the profit margins anymore; rather, we take into account values such as fairness, compassion, and an eye toward the impact it will have on eternity.

Aspirations, Modesty, and a Sense of Purpose

A desire for expansion and ambition are both necessary components of successful investing. Nevertheless, the goal of the Christian investor is essentially distinct from the ambition of the rest of the world. It is accompanied by a profound sense of humility, as well as a distinct awareness of the divine purpose.

According to the verse found in James 4:6, "God opposes the proud but shows favor to the humble." Our objective is not to further our own interests, but rather to forward the cause of God's kingdom. Everything that we do, from the investments that we make to the tactics that we use to the risks that we take, is evaluated in light of God's everlasting plans and our position as His servants.

Our journey of investing becomes led by a vision of God's goodness and our responsibility in extending that goodness to other people as a result of this balance between ambition and humility, which transforms our trip into a spiritual activity.

The world of finance is a complicated one, replete with a variety of opportunities, hazards, and constantly shifting landscapes. To navigate this terrain successfully, you need wisdom and judgment, both of which are traits that the Bible praises in a variety of different chapters.

It is said in the book of Proverbs that "blessed is the one who finds wisdom, and the one who gets understanding." We seek wisdom via prayer, through the guidance of godly mentors, and through a continuing commitment to learning and improving in our understanding of the world and ourselves. The decisions we make about our investments are not independent business choices; rather, they are intricately intertwined with our faith, our morals, and the work we are called to do. We recognize that our success is not just a consequence of our talent or plan, but rather a reflection of God's supply and blessing. As a result, we depend on God for guidance, and we are aware that our success is not simply a product of our skill or strategy.

Investing is a spiritual calling as much as it is a plan for making money in the market. When viewed through the prism of faith, each choice we make about our investments becomes a reflection of our relationship with God, our confidence in His supply, and our dedication to furthering His objectives.

It is encouraged in verses 17-19 of 1 Timothy chapter 6 that we should not put our hope in riches but rather in God, "being rich in good deeds, and to be generous and willing to share."

Our investments are not only financial tools; rather, they are instruments of grace. They are conduits through which the love, provision, and justice of God flow out into the world. Our financial contributions, whether they go toward providing educational opportunities for those who are economically disadvantaged or creating jobs that preserve human dignity, are channels through which God's kingdom might be advanced here on earth.

When approached from a Christian worldview, the process of investing can be transformed into an exciting and meaningful spiritual adventure. It raises the discussion above merely discussing numbers and strategy to a level where we can discuss timeless principles and divine callings.

When we focus our thoughts on things that are above, we bring our investing journey into alignment with the heart of God. We acknowledge that He is the owner of all, we accept His purpose, we seek His wisdom, and we respond to His calling.

No longer is our accomplishment measured by the standards of this world; rather, it is measured by the everlasting measurements of loyalty, impact, and alignment with the kingdom of God.

When viewed through the lens of one's faith, the attitude of an investor is a deep and multifaceted perspective that rises above concerns of this world and embraces principles that will last forever. It's not just about the monetary gain; it's also about the spiritual development, the impact on God's kingdom, and the delight of collaborating with God in His work of redemption.

May our journey through the world of investing be an ongoing practice in focusing our eyes on things that are above, guided by God's wisdom, motivated by His love, and always focused on the eternal treasures that moth and rust cannot destroy. Because Christ provides us with the genuine purpose, joy, and success of investing, as well as a means to honoring God, helping others, and fulfilling our divine calling, we are able to find all of these things in the process of investing.

Overcoming Challenges: Perseverance and Trust in God

Investing in real estate is a multidimensional effort that requires not just a sound understanding of finance but also a healthy spirit that is filled with faith and tenacity. It is a field in which one should always be prepared for the unexpected, and the difficulties that arise as a result of the unexpected can either turn away those who lack courage or shape those who face them with faith and resolve.

Finding Joy in Difficult Circumstances

James 1:2-4 does not only encourage us, but rather mandates that we rejoice in our tribulations. This makes little sense, especially in the cutthroat business of real estate, where competition is fierce. This joy, however, originates from the realization that the testing of our faith results in a perseverance that ultimately leads to the development of spiritual maturity. Every obstacle we face along the way to being successful investors can be reframed as opportunities bestowed by God to deepen our relationship with Him, mature our faith in Him, and cultivate a character that brings glory to Him.

Imagine working your way through a challenging real estate transaction, where there are roadblocks at every turn. The attitude of someone who is not filled with faith, on the other hand, may be one of irritation or despair, but someone who is filled with faith will recognize the hand of God at work, purifying, teaching, and directing them.

The Kind of Endurance That Molds Character

Investing is not for those who are easily discouraged. There will be challenges, obstacles, and losses along the way. Our comprehension of persistence is deepened by Romans 5:3–4 because the passage establishes a connection between it and the formation of character and hope. The tenacity that we cultivate by successfully navigating the obstacles presented by investing decisions molds our personalities, makes us more resilient, and establishes us in the hope that does not let us down.

We are not only surviving the hardships; rather, we are thriving through them and growing into the likeness of Christ, who endured all things for the joy that was set before Him (Hebrews 12:2).

Placing Belief in the Supreme Authority of God

There is no financial strategy that can account for every conceivable outcome. The economic climate is subject to change, and unanticipated occurrences have the potential to derail even the most meticulously crafted strategies. These are the times that test our ability to maintain control, but they also present us with wonderful opportunity to believe in the omnipotence of God.

This presents an opportunity to put the words of Proverbs 3:5-6 into effect, leaning not on our own understanding but rather yielding to the wisdom of God. This trust implies acknowledging that God is the ultimate owner of everything we have, and that He is the one who is orchestrating events for both our benefit and His glory. This is especially important in the realm of real estate.

Drawing Inspiration and Courage from the Promises of God

Having the fortitude, determination, and courage to continue investing in real estate is essential, particularly when one is confronted with discouraging conditions. It is in times like these that the promises of God shine brightest as a lighthouse of encouragement and hope.

We are able to face obstacles with renewed vitality, wisdom, and grace because of promises such as Isaiah 40:31, which tell us that our strength does not come from our ability but rather from our hope in the Lord.

A Helping and Caring Community

The process of investing doesn't necessarily have to be a lonesome one. The New Testament describes a thriving community of believers who uplift and pray for one another and share in the responsibilities of caring for one another's needs. You should give some thought to surrounding yourself with godly mentors, financial advisors who share your religion, and fellow investors who can offer prayer and encouragement. It is not enough to simply have a sound financial strategy or strong business acumen in order to be successful in real estate investing. It is a profoundly spiritual journey that presents possibilities to grow in one's dependency on God, as well as one's faith and character.

We begin to realize that trials should not be viewed as impediments, but rather as openings through which we might grow closer to God, experience the reliability of God, and more closely resemble Christ.

Our perseverance is not a result of our own power, but rather a demonstration of the grace of God at work within each one of us. Our success is not just judged in terms of revenues and returns; rather, it is determined by our spiritual growth, our fidelity, and how well we align ourselves with God's intentions. May we approach each decision about investments with an eternal perspective, a trusting heart, and a resilient spirit, knowing that in all things, God works for the good of those who love Him and who have been called according to His purpose (Romans 8:28). In this journey, we are never alone; we have the promises of God, the guidance of His Word, and the fellowship of His people to encourage, support, and direct us toward an investment path that glorifies Him and benefits others. In addition, we have the fellowship of His people.

Embracing Growth and Learning: Growing in Wisdom and Stature

Investing is not just a means to financial success; rather, it is also a way to cultivate one's spirituality and personal growth. As we delve further into the myriad components of maturing in both wisdom and stature, we unearth significant truths that bring us into alignment with God's purpose, mold who we are as people, and expand the sphere of our influence in the world.

The Quest for Wisdom as an Ongoing Activity

According to Proverbs 9:10, the first step in gaining wisdom is to have a healthy fear of the Lord. This is an endeavor that never ends. This insight is an insight that comes from a close relationship with God, directing our investment choices and plans. This wisdom exceeds ordinary knowledge; it is an insight that emanates from a close relationship with God. Solomon's wisdom, who was famed for his insight, reminds us that we should pray to God for wisdom regarding our financial decisions. His request for wisdom resulted in a just and prudent reign over Israel, giving an example for us to seek God's guidance in the choices we make with our investments (1 Kings 3:5-14).

Lessons can be gained through experiences, whether they are successful or not. They mold our plans, hone our judgments, and direct our investments in a way that is congruent with our spiritual convictions. When we contemplate these events with a heart that is tuned in to the voice of God, we are able to obtain insights that are not only practically useful but also spiritually enlightening.

Standing: The Integrity to Influence Relationship

Gaining stature entails more than just establishing one's reputation or achieving one's goals. It is about having the same character as Christ in how we do our business with money.

Our investment activities are to be carried out in accordance with the highest standards of honesty, fairness, and integrity. Not only does this integrity help to develop trust, but it also testifies to the faith that we have in Christ (Proverbs 11:3). Our commitment to integrity speaks volumes about our faith, whether it is in the form of upholding agreements, treating tenants with respect, or ensuring that our investments correspond with ethical principles.

The Power to Influence and Its Effects

Our investments are not only monetary activities in isolation; rather, they have the capacity to influence communities, provide support for missions, and reflect the love of God. Because we are stewards of the resources that belong to God, we have the ability to use our money to support causes that are close to God's heart, so expanding the scope of our influence beyond the realm of finance (Matthew 5:13-16).

Education Throughout a Lifetime: Spiritual Enlightenment and Economic Mastery

The ever-changing landscape of the investment world necessitates a never-ending dedication to professional development and education.

It is necessary to maintain one's level of education on financial principles, market trends, and investing techniques. We need to devote a lot of effort into acquiring the experience and education that will allow us to make intelligent choices regarding our investments.

Spiritual Development and Growth

Our relationship with God must serve as the bedrock upon which we build our maturation in both wisdom and stature. Praying and studying the Bible on a daily basis, as well as having a spiritual guide, helps create a heart that is attentive to God's direction and that views business prospects through the prism of faith.

The path toward growth and learning in the field of investment is one that is challenging but ultimately rewarding. Our efforts should not be limited to merely monetary activities but should also be spiritual endeavors that reflect our faith in Christ as we continue to grow in wisdom and stature.

It is about leveraging our influence for God's glory, aligning our investments with God's ideals, reflecting His character in our interactions, and continuously growing and adapting in a world that is always changing.

Our investments should be more than just transactions; they should be transformational, bringing us closer to God, forming our character, and having an impact on the world in ways that bring glory to Him. Let's begin this path of investment with hearts that are receptive to the wisdom that God has to provide, lives that are committed to integrity, and minds that are engaged to learning and growing throughout life. If we follow this course of action, we will discover a road that not only leads to material success, but also to spiritual fulfillment and enduring significance.

Staying Motivated: Running the Race with Perseverance

How to Maintain Your Motivation and Keep Going When Things Get Tough

Investing is not only a form of financial activity or a route to amassing individual wealth. It's a spiritual version of running a marathon, a long-haul trip filled with ups and downs, challenges and victories. However, it is precisely in this race that we find the profound potential for spiritual development, personal growth, and an intimate relationship with the purpose that God has for our life.

Having the perspective that investing is a greater calling elevates what would otherwise be a commonplace activity to the level of a heavenly mission. It's not only about making money or losing money; it's about being a good steward of God's resources by acting with honesty, knowledge, and faith. The motive that drives us to compete in this race goes beyond merely gaining ephemeral benefits and instead is in line with eternal values. We are not racing without a destination in mind, but rather with a specific objective in mind that represents God's plan and will for our lives.

Taking an investment strategy that is driven by a meaningful purpose enables us to look beyond the short-term fluctuations of the market. We are commanded to move forward with purpose, taking our cue from the life of Jesus, who "for the joy set before him he endured the cross, scorning its shame" (Hebrews 12:2). When we are led by a distinct and Christ-centered vision, not only may our investment journey be filled with joy, but it can also be defined by endurance.

Investing according to Christian principles is predicated on faith. Trusting our tactics or the market is only part of the equation; more importantly, we must also trust in God's sovereignty over everything. Because of this trust, we are released from anxiety, given the fortitude to endure, and given the ability to perceive God's hand in every step of the investing path that we are on.

The Importance of Motivation, Community, and Being Accountable

Maintaining one's perseverance throughout the marathon is not intended to be a solo activity. We are commanded to encircle ourselves with a community of other Christians, mentors, and friends who are capable of supplying us with encouragement, wisdom, and accountability. Because of this communal facet, our relationship with others and with God is strengthened, which not only makes the trip more tolerable but also more joyous and meaningful.

Overcoming Challenges and Gaining Knowledge from One's Errors

The competition in the world of investments is fraught with challenges, reverses, and even occasional defeats. Nevertheless, they are not setbacks but rather opportunities to learn, mature, and get closer to God through our relationship with him. We have the ability to transform these obstacles into stepping stones on the path to more wisdom and a deeper faith if we are tenacious and maintain a good mindset.

An Eternal Point of View

The real end point of our race to become wealthy is not when we reach our financial goal or retire; rather, it is the moment when we must give an account to God of how we have conducted ourselves throughout the race. The words "Well done, good and faithful servant" are the greatest honor and the eternal award that provides value and purpose to all of our endeavors. These words are also the recompense that we will get in eternity.

The race of investing is a holy adventure, comparable to running a marathon with endurance, faith, and an unyielding concentration on Christ. It is a journey that enlightens us, molds us, and ultimately brings us nearer to the very center of God's being.

We pray that we will be able to run this course with grace and enthusiasm, with our sights set on the prize that will last forever and our hearts ablaze with a desire for the Kingdom of God. May we not only engage our financial resources but also our whole lives in this great journey, knowing that each step, each decision, and each victory is an opportunity to glorify God and become more like Christ. May we do so with the understanding that we can become more like Christ through participating in each of these events.

The distance is far, the obstacles are difficult, but the prize is unrivaled in its significance. Run with perseverance, invest with integrity, and live with an eternal perspective, for the race is not for the swift but for those who run in faith, relying in God's grace, and living for His glory. So run the race with these three things in mind: run with perseverance, invest with integrity, and live with an eternal perspective.

The importance of maintaining a positive attitude and remaining resilient via faith

As Christians who engage in real estate, we start on a journey that goes well beyond the world of monetary advancement and the accumulation of assets. This journey is about so much more. This voyage will take you through the difficult terrains of faith, character, spiritual growth, and most importantly, thinking. The mindset of an investor is the rudder that helps us navigate the unpredictability of the real estate market. Knowledge, patience, a positive attitude, and the ability to persevere are the four ingredients that, when combined, will determine our course of action and our level of success.

Positive Thinking as a Mental Attitude

At first glance, it may appear that positivity is a relatively secular feature of our frame of mind, something that would be more at home in a motivational speech than in an exposition on the bible. However, as we go deeper into the meaning of what it means to be positive for a Christian, we come to see that it is a reflection of our confidence and trust in the promises that God has made. It is the hope-filled optimism that results from trusting the words of Jeremiah 29:11, which read, "For I know the plans I have for you, declares the Lord, plans for welfare and not for evil, to give you a future and a hope."

Positivity enables us to perceive possibilities where others see hurdles, and it gives the resilience necessary to weather the natural risks and challenges that come with the investment experience. This optimism, on the other hand, is not founded on nothing more than wishful thinking or naiveté. It is a heavenly positivism that is grounded on the promises of God, which do not change. It is a reassurance that God is at work, that He has a plan, and that He is able to work all things together for our good (Romans 8:28). Even when we are going through difficult times, God is working on our behalf.

The capacity to persevere in the face of adversity is referred to as resilience.

Another essential component of the mindset of an investor is resilience, which is especially important in a sector as volatile as real estate. It is the capacity to pick ourselves up when we fall, to continue with tenacity even when the going gets tough, and to persevere in spite of the obstacles and defeats that we encounter.

The biblical concept of resilience, on the other hand, is not the same as worldly grit or determination. It's the sort of resiliency that comes from our faith; it's the kind of resiliency that echoes the spirit of the Apostle Paul, who wrote in 2 Corinthians 4:8-9, "We are hard-pressed on every side, but not crushed; perplexed, but not in despair; persecuted, but not abandoned; struck down, but not destroyed." This is the kind of resiliency that flows from our faith.

The Christian Investor's Firm Foundation is Their Faith

Faith serves as the very foundational component of the attitude of a Christian investor. It's about coming to terms with the fact that even while we put in the effort—doing research, devising plans, and weighing our options—in the end, it is God who determines who will be successful. Faith is about shedding the load of anxiety and resting in the confidence that God is sovereign over every investment decision and every market outcome. It also involves giving up the illusion of control that one has over one's circumstances.

Developing a Spiritual Attitude Towards Investing

The question now is, how can we develop this mentality? To begin, it is necessary to be intentional, to pray, and to completely immerse oneself in the Word of God. It is imperative that we make it a priority to cultivate an attitude of thankfulness, contentment, and a heart that is intent on giving God glory in every facet of our lives. It requires a commitment to lifelong education, an attitude that is teachable and receptive to guidance and instruction, as well as the bravery to venture beyond of our comfort zones.

We are reminded that the size of our portfolio or the amount of money in our bank accounts is not the only factor that determines how successful we are as real estate investors as we navigate the treacherous yet rewarding path of real estate investing. Our success as Christian investors is a reflection of our mindset, which is shown in our positivity, our resilience, our steadfast faith, and our unrelenting resolve to glorify God in every step that we take.

As we move forward, let us not forget that the purpose of our investing journey is not only to acquire homes or assets; rather, it is to further the cause of God's kingdom. Let us devote our time, energy, and resources to accomplishing God's will so that His name will be praised. Let's instill faith and honesty into every investment decision we make.

We began this chapter by setting out on a journey to explore the fundamentals of the thinking of a Christian investor. This investigation has led us to delve more deeply into the core of our faith as well as the ways in which it interacts with our investment strategy.

To begin, we came to an awareness of the significance of keeping our thoughts focused on things that are above, and we reminded ourselves that our job as investors is simply to steward God's wealth in a manner that is submissive, charitable, and driven by a higher purpose. As Christian investors, our attitude must be oriented toward eternal truths and directed by divine wisdom from the very beginning of our investing careers.

After that, we worked our way through the minefield of obstacles and tests that is inherent in the world of investing. Here, we discovered that our perseverance is not just a measure of our tenacity but also a testimonial to our trust in God's sovereignty and goodness. This was a profound realization for us. The more adversity we go through, the more of a chance we are presented with to grow in our relationship with God, to become more developed on our spiritual path, and to demonstrate his glory to others via our ability to persevere.

Following that, our inquiry brought to our attention the significance of ongoing education and development. We have a responsibility, both as investors and as followers of Christ, to grow continually in understanding, stature, and spiritual maturity. The world of finance provides a one-of-a-kind educational opportunity to learn not only about various financial strategies and market trends, but also about one's own identity, values, and the divine calling to which one has been called.

In order to keep one's motivation up during the course of this extended voyage, one must have the determination and the fortitude to run the marathon with unwavering dedication. In the same way that our spiritual path is a marathon and not a sprint, the race of investing is also a marathon. It demands perseverance, a viewpoint that looks forward, and the wisdom to keep our eyes fixed on the final finish line, which is the eternal reward we are working toward.

At last, we took a more in-depth look at the importance of remaining optimistic and resilient in the face of adversity. These are attributes that are essential to a good investor's thinking. This optimism, which has its origins in the confidence and trust that we have in God, gives us the strength to recognize opportunities where other people see problems. This resilience provides us with the fuel to rise to the challenge of difficult situations and to endure in the face of failure.

It is important to keep in mind that as Christian investors, we are in a unique position to bring glory to God by the decisions and acts that we take about our investments. Our frame of mind and strategy for investing are demonstrations of our faith, honesty, and dedication to the advancement of God's kingdom. And so, as we make our way through this adventure that is real estate investing, let us do it with a heart that is fixed on God, a mind that is centered on faith, and a spirit that is filled with positivity and the ability to persevere. The path may be difficult and riddled with obstacles, but if we have God as our leader and faith as our basis, we will be able to navigate it with assurance, a sense of purpose, and hope for a future that will bring glory to God and fulfill the purposes of His kingdom.

Your Real Estate Journey

Looking Back: Gratitude and Lessons Learned

As we now turn our attention to the past, we will proceed to retrace our steps through the immersive world of faith-based real estate investing by going down the corridors of each chapter that we have already investigated. It is time to take a moment to halt, collect our thoughts, and consider the magnificent adventure that we have traveled together up until this point.

Every new chapter unfurled in front of us like a tapestry, expertly stitched with strands of biblical truths, strategic investment strategies, and priceless life lessons. Each thread is more than just a strand of knowledge; rather, they are stepping stones that bring us to a profound intersection where faith and finances can be brought together in a concordant manner.

This journey that we set out on together went well beyond the realms of monetary gain and material possessions to encompass something much more intangible. It explored the spiritual realms of personal development, comprehension, and enlightenment as a means of achieving its goals. We learned deeper truths about the essence of stewardship, the power of resilience, and the unrelenting strength of faith with every success that we celebrated and every setback that we overcame.

Let us now, as we stand at the intersection of introspection and action, open our hearts to the feeling of appreciation. Permit it to sweep over us, allowing it to touch every memory, every lesson that we've learned, and every moment of illumination. Every step we've made on this road, every nugget of insight we've gained, and every obstacle we've triumphed over is a resolute demonstration of God's unwavering leadership and unfathomable grace, and they all serve as a lasting monument to these truths.

So, let's not just try to recall what we've learned here. Instead, let us make them a part of who we are by allowing them to leave an impression on our hearts and allowing them to mold and direct the path that lies ahead of us. In this place, in this state of deep reflection and heartfelt thanks, we are able to fully appreciate the development we've cultivated, the insights we've uncovered, and the trip we've taken in the light of God's unchanging wisdom.

Looking Forward: Hope and Faith for the Future

As we find ourselves on the brink of the next leg of our adventure in real estate investment, we halt for a moment and cast our gaze towards the horizon, which glimmers with the possibilities of the future. It is an invitation to move on with unshakable hope and unwavering trust, both of which are deeply entrenched and firmly anchored in the truth of God's unchanging promises and the unchanging essence of God himself.

The journey that we have started is more than just an investigation of different investment methods and fundamentals of the financial world. It is a spiritual voyage, a pilgrimage guided by the blazing light of God's Word, through the landscapes of life and towards our eternal home. This journey will take place over the course of one's lifetime. Each move that we have made has been directed by the compass of heavenly wisdom, and we have drawn both inspiration and direction from the words of Proverbs chapter three verses five and six: "Trust in the LORD with all your heart, and do not lean on your own understanding; in all your ways submit to Him, and He will make your paths straight." (Proverbs 3:5-6) "Trust in the LORD with all your heart."

We have realized that putting our faith in God is of incomparable worth, not only as the cornerstone of our investment plan, but also as the cornerstone of our lives. This realization has come about as a result of all that we have learned, which includes the study of biblical principles as well as a grasp of the complexities of investing.

Let us carry this heavenly promise like a beacon within our hearts as we get ready to stride forward towards the dawn of untold potential. With this holy confidence serving as our amulet of faith, we submit our agendas to His will, put our faith in His divine providence, and attune our brains to the frequency of His kingdom.

We do not move forward into the future on our own, but rather in a divine partnership, walking hand in hand with God, the Almighty, who serves as our leader, our teacher, and our compass. Because of our trust in Him, we are able to face the unpredictability of the future with confidence, because we know that no matter what the future holds, He has us safely ensconced in the palm of His hand.

As we turn each page in our quest to become successful real estate investors, let us remember the biblical truths of stewardship, the value of faith-infused ambition, the strength of endurance, and the transformative impact of having a mindset that is focused on God. Every success, every struggle that is surmounted, and every lesson that is learned ought to lead us back to the One who dictates our course and guides our feet.

When we look ahead, let us not forget that our faith and hope for the future are not merely about our success in real estate investing; rather, they are about our progress as disciples of Christ, stewards of God's resources, and lights in this world. Let us not forget this fact as we move forward. The way that lies ahead of us is not simply a highway leading to material wealth; rather, it is a trip towards spiritual plenty, with Christ serving as our final goal.

Final Words of Wisdom: Navigating the Real Estate World with Faith

Let us pause for a brief time and take some deep breaths as we make our way through the final pages of our adventure together. We have set out on an illuminating journey across the intricate terrain of real estate investing, and throughout this journey, we will continue to keep our compass pointed in the direction provided by the Holy Scriptures. Our mission has involved more than just the accumulation of knowledge concerning business dealings, market conditions, or strategic planning. It has been a journey toward the core of wisdom, the kind of wisdom that molds personality, strengthens faith, and offers a compass that is useful much beyond the confines of the real estate industry.

Along the way, we have realized that our connection with God is the most important aspect of any form of investment. In spite of the tides that constantly move the market, this is one truth that will never be shaken or moved. As was covered in Chapter 2, the value of the actual things that we accumulate, such as our property and investment portfolios, may rise and fall over time, but the consistency of God's faithfulness will never alter.

In addition, we have seen that putting our faith in God's omnipotence serves as the rudder that guides us through the waves of uncertainty. As we saw in Chapter 4, economic unpredictability and market volatility may appear to be significant challenges; nevertheless, when evaluated in the context of divine sovereignty, these challenges appear to be less intimidating. Keep in mind that God's hand is guiding the universe, and that He is more than capable of leading you through the process of buying or selling real estate.

And whenever you find yourself in the midst of storms, whenever the problems threaten to overwhelm you, let faith be your shield and endurance your weapon. Think back on the things you learned in Chapter 6. Confront these challenges with a mindset that can not only remain resilient but also find joy in the midst of difficult circumstances. Embrace the process of refinement, for it is through this process that our faith is tried, and it is through this process that our endurance is strengthened.

In the chapters that followed, we discussed why it is critical for us to maintain a state of perpetual growth and education throughout our investment journey. The need of having other skills in addition to strong financial knowledge was underlined in Chapter 7. It necessitates the development of one's spiritual maturity, one's ethical integrity, and one's capacity to see beyond the bottom line of one's finances. Take the advice presented here to heart as you move forward in the realm of real estate.

However, even the most accurate map or the most reliable compass cannot ensure that the travel will be straightforward. Keep in mind the metaphor of the race that was introduced in Chapter 8. The process of investing is similar to running a marathon and takes perseverance. As you continue on your road, keep in mind to "run with perseverance the race marked out for us," investing with an eye not just on the transient gains of this world but also on the rewards that will last forever.

In essence, when we come to the end of this book, it is my hope and prayer for you that the advice that is included within these pages won't just stay as words on a page. Instead, I hope that you will take these lessons to heart and let them serve as guiding principles for you as you navigate the world of real estate and beyond. Keep in mind that when God is in charge of your life, you are in a position to make choices that not only benefit you monetarily but also have an impact on the rest of your life eternally. After all, at the end of the day, our ultimate goal is not just to be great investors but also to be faithful stewards of the benefits that God has provided for us. As a result, as we get to the end of this book, I want you to go off on your trip with a sense of enthusiasm and eagerness.

Keep these ideas close to your heart, and allow them to direct your actions moving forward. Move forward with the knowledge that God, who has led you through this learning journey, will also continue to lead you through the process of buying and selling real estate. It is imperative that you constantly maintain your religion at the forefront of everything you do while you navigate the fascinating world of investment. Although the market may experience fluctuations, the promises of God do not change. If you maintain your steadfastness in those assurances, you will discover that the years ahead are filled with hope, faith, and opportunity.

An Ongoing Journey with Christ at the Center

We have now reached the close of this enlightening exploration, but as we turn the final pages of this book, we find ourselves standing not at the end, but at the beginning of a new and exciting chapter. Emboldened by the insights and wisdom we've garnered, we are poised to set forth into the vibrant world of faith-based real estate investing. Yet, as we step forward, we do so knowing that our exploration does not conclude here, for our journey is ongoing, ever guided by the irreplaceable light of Christ's teachings.

We began this journey together by acknowledging an essential truth that echoed across every chapter of this book: our financial endeavors and spiritual faith are not parallel paths but interconnected aspects of our lives. This principle formed the bedrock of our journey, presenting us with a unique lens to view real estate investing, not just as a financial venture, but as a spiritual mission of stewardship that expands our understanding of faith.

Recall how, in Chapter 1, we established Christ as the cornerstone of all our endeavors, including our investments. The roadmap for our decisions should not be restricted to worldly metrics of success, but ought to encompass and be guided by the love and teachings of Jesus Christ.

The journey led us through the peaks and valleys of risk and reward in Chapter 3, affirming the notion that faith-based investing is not about evading risks, but embracing them with courage and wisdom. We wield the shield of trust in God's guidance, knowing it to be our strength in navigating through the tumultuous seas of investment decisions.

In Chapter 5, we took a deep dive into the world of real estate negotiation, a realm that is as dynamic as it is challenging. Here, we discovered that our actions and decisions should always echo Christian principles of fairness, honesty, and love for our neighbors.

Subsequent chapters introduced us to the concept of resilience, growth, and perseverance. Our walk through real estate investing is not a smooth path devoid of hurdles, but it is these very challenges that offer us opportunities to grow in faith, fortify our patience, and refine our character.

Throughout this journey, we have interwoven the strands of faith and investing to create a comprehensive tapestry that depicts a clear picture of faith-based real estate investing. The principles, strategies, and lessons are not only relevant to this sector but permeate all facets of our life journey, illuminating our path with the brilliant light of biblical wisdom.

Thus, as we close this chapter, let's remember: our journey in real estate investing is part of a broader, richer tapestry—our walk with God. This walk doesn't exist in isolation—it is inextricably intertwined with our spiritual journey. Our exploration continues, with Christ as the guiding star, His teachings our compass, and our faith, the wind in our sails.

As we step onto the path that lies ahead, let's strive to apply what we've learned. Let these principles guide us, let them inform our decisions, and let them shape our mindset. Above all, let us keep our gaze firmly fixed on Christ, our unfaltering guide and companion.

May your continued journey be filled with growth, resilience, and God's bountiful blessings. As you venture further into the realm of real estate investing, remember to always keep faith at your core, let Christ guide your course, and ensure your journey glorifies God. This ongoing journey, like our faith, is a living testament to God's work in our lives. Godspeed on your journey, and may His grace be with you every step of the way.

Work book

Chapter 1: Stewardship and Investing

Exercise 1.1: Write down what stewardship means to you in the context of your personal finance and real estate investing.
Exercise 1.2: List three ways in which you could implement better stewardship principles in your current investing strategy.
Reflection Question 1.1: How do you perceive your role as a steward in real estate investing?
Reflection Question 1.2: Can you recall a situation where you've exemplified the principles of stewardship in your investing?
Journal Section 1.1: Reflect on how stewardship has already played a role in your investing journey.

Journal Section 1.2: Write about how you plan to apply the principle of stewardship to your future investment plans.

Note:

Chapter 2: The Investment Mindset: A Spiritual Perspective

Exercise 2.1: Write down 3 ways you can incorporate your faith into your investment mindset.

Exercise 2.2: Identify and write down a scripture verse that resonates with you about faith and finances. Reflect on why this verse speaks to you.

Reflection Question 2.1: How can your faith guide your decision-making process in real estate investing?

Reflection Question 2.2: Can you recall a moment where your faith significantly influenced an investment decision?

Journal Section 2.1: Reflect on how your faith has influenced your investment mindset thus far.

Journal Section 2.2: Write about any changes you may need to make in your current investing mindset to align it more closely with your faith.

Exercise 3.1: List three key indicators you look for when identifying a promising real estate investment opportunity. Reflect on how these indicators align with your faith-based approach to investing.

Exercise 3.2: Think about a risk you've taken in real estate investing. Was it a calculated risk? How did your faith influence this decision?

Exercise 3.3: Recount a time when you declined an opportunity because it didn't align with your faith-based principles. How did you feel about this decision, and what did you learn?

Reflection Question 3.1: In what ways can your faith guide you in identifying the right opportunities and evaluating the associated risks in real estate investing?

Reflection Question 3.2: How do you balance faith with practical considerations when dealing with risks in real estate investing?

Journal Section 3.1: Reflect on your experiences in recognising opportunities and taking risks in real estate investing. Write about a specific instance when your faith played a significant role in making a decision.

Journal Section 3.2: Looking to the future, how do you plan to incorporate your faith more into your decision-making process for recognising opportunities and handling risks?

Note:

_____

_____

Remember that the exercises, reflection questions, and journal sections are all designed to foster a deeper understanding of how faith can guide real estate investing. They provide a personal space for readers to consider their unique circumstances and experiences, promoting a more profound application of the principles discussed in each chapter.

Chapter 4: Diversifying Your Portfolio: Many Advisers Make Victory Sure

Exercise 4.1: Review your current investment portfolio. Is it diversified? If not, list three ways you can diversify your portfolio that aligns with your Christian values.

Exercise 4.2: Identify three trusted advisers who could offer different perspectives on your investment strategy. These can be spiritual advisers, financial advisers, or trusted family and friends.

Exercise 4.3: Reflect on a time when you made a decision based on the advice of multiple advisers. How did this advice help you avoid pitfalls or seize opportunities?

Reflection Question 4.1: How do the principles of diversification align with biblical teachings?

Reflection Question 4.2: How has seeking the counsel of many advisers benefited your investment strategy?

Journal Section 4.1: Write about a time when diversification or the lack of it significantly impacted your investment outcome. How did your faith guide you in this situation?

Journal Section 4.2: Looking forward, how do you plan to implement biblical principles of diversification and counsel in your investment strategy?

Note:

_____

_____

These exercises, reflection questions, and journal prompts are meant to encourage you to apply the principles discussed in Chapter 4 to your own investing journey. Reflecting on your personal experiences can give you valuable insights into how these principles work in practice and how you can continue to grow in your faith-based investing approach.

Exercise 5.1: Identify three potential risks that could impact your investment portfolio. Consider market fluctuations, specific property issues, or broader economic factors.

Exercise 5.2: For each risk identified in Exercise 5.1, develop a strategy to mitigate or manage that risk.

Exercise 5.3: Evaluate your current portfolio. Are there investments that are not protected or shielded from potential risks? If so, how can you rectify this?

Reflection Question 5.1: How does the biblical principle of stewardship inform the way you approach risk management in your portfolio?

Reflection Question 5.2: What are some key learnings about portfolio protection that you've gleaned from this chapter? How do these align with your faith and values?

Journal Section 5.1: Reflect on a time when a risk you hadn't considered affected your investments. How did you respond, and how did your faith inform your reaction?

Journal Section 5.2: Moving forward, how do you plan to better protect your portfolio while upholding your Christian principles?

Note:

_____

_____

These exercises, reflection questions, and journal prompts are designed to help you apply the principles of risk management and portfolio protection to your investing journey. Use these prompts to reflect on your current strategy and how you might improve it in the future. Reflecting on your experiences can provide invaluable insights for your future investing decisions.

Chapter 6: Maintaining Your Portfolio: The Faithful Steward

Exercise 6.1: Take a comprehensive look at your portfolio. Are there areas that could use better maintenance or more focused attention?

Exercise 6.2: Identify three ways you could improve the ongoing management of your portfolio. This might include new tools, habits, or practices.

Exercise 6.3: Consider a property in your portfolio that requires significant maintenance. Develop a detailed plan for addressing these needs while considering cost-effectiveness and long-term sustainability.

Reflection Question 6.1: What does faithful stewardship look like in the context of your investment portfolio?

Reflection Question 6.2: Reflect on the biblical principles discussed in this chapter. How have they influenced your perspective on maintaining your real estate portfolio?

Journal Section 6.1: Write about a time when you successfully maintained or improved an aspect of your portfolio. What made this experience a success?

Journal Section 6.2: Reflect on an aspect of portfolio maintenance that you find challenging. How might you improve in this area, guided by your faith?

Note:

_____

_____

Chapter 7: Expanding Your Portfolio: A Good Measure, Pressed Down, Shaken Together, and Running Over

Exercise 7.1: Identify three possible ways to expand your portfolio that align with your investment strategy and Christian values.

Exercise 7.2: For each expansion opportunity identified in Exercise 7.1, conduct a brief analysis of the potential benefits and drawbacks.

Exercise 7.3: Draft a plan to pursue one of the expansion opportunities identified in Exercise 7.1. Consider all necessary steps, resources needed, and potential challenges.

Reflection Question 7.1: What are some key factors to consider when expanding your portfolio, based on the biblical principles discussed in this chapter?

Reflection Question 7.2: How do the concepts of generosity and abundance shape your approach to expanding your portfolio?

Journal Section 7.1: Reflect on a time when you expanded your portfolio. How did this align with your faith and values?

Journal Section 7.2: Consider your future goals for expanding your portfolio. How do these align with your faith and your role as a steward of God's resources?

Note:

_____

_____

These exercises, reflection questions, and journal prompts are intended to engage you in thoughtful consideration of your portfolio's maintenance and expansion. Take the time to reflect on each question and jot down your thoughts, experiences, and future plans.

Exercise 8.1: Evaluate the current protections you have in place for your real estate portfolio. Are there any gaps or vulnerabilities?

Exercise 8.2: Research three additional protective measures you could implement for your portfolio.

Exercise 8.3: Create a detailed plan to implement one of the protective measures identified in Exercise 8.2. This should include a timeline, necessary resources, and the expected impact.

Reflection Question 8.1: How does the biblical principle of prudence inform your approach to protecting your real estate investments?

Reflection Question 8.2: How can you balance reliance on God's providence with the wise, proactive protection of your investments?

Journal Section 8.1: Reflect on a time when you implemented a protective measure for your portfolio. What were the results?

Journal Section 8.2: Consider a vulnerability in your portfolio. How might you address this using wisdom and prudence?

Note:

Exercise 9.1: Conduct a thorough review of your portfolio. What areas are performing well? Where might there be room for improvement?

Exercise 9.2: Set SMART (Specific, Measurable, Achievable, Relevant, Time-bound) goals for the next quarter based on your portfolio review.

Exercise 9.3: Create a regular schedule for portfolio reviews. Consider how often these reviews should occur and what they should entail.

Reflection Question 9.1: What role do wisdom and humility play in the review and assessment of your portfolio?

Reflection Question 9.2: How can you use portfolio reviews as opportunities for prayer and reflection, not just strategic planning?

Journal Section 9.1: Write about a significant insight or lesson learned from a past portfolio review.

Journal Section 9.2: Consider your goals for the future of your portfolio. How do these reflect your faith and values as a Christian investor?

Note:

_____

_____

Each of these exercises, reflection questions, and journal prompts should guide your contemplation and application of the principles discussed in these chapters. Your honest engagement will deepen your understanding and practice of faith-informed real estate investing.

Chapter 10: The Investor Mindset: Maintaining a Christ-Centered Perspective

Exercise 10.1: Reflect on your own investor mindset. How does it align with the Christ-centered mindset described in this chapter?

Exercise 10.2: Identify three practical ways you can cultivate a more Christ-centered mindset in your investing activities.

Exercise 10.3: Write a personal mission statement for your investing that reflects a Christ-centered mindset.

Reflection Question 10.1: How does maintaining a Christ-centered mindset impact your investing strategies and decisions?

Reflection Question 10.2: How can you encourage and uphold a Christ-centered investor mindset in challenging times?

Journal Section 10.1: Share a time when your investor mindset positively affected an investing decision or outcome.

Journal Section 10.2: Reflect on potential areas of growth in aligning your investor mindset more closely with your faith.

Note:

_____

_____

Final Thoughts: Your Real Estate Journey

Exercise FT.1: Reflect on your key takeaways from this book. How have they changed your approach to real estate investing?

Exercise FT.2: Outline a plan to implement these takeaways into your real estate investing strategy.

Exercise FT.3: Identify three goals for your real estate journey that are grounded in the principles you've learned from this book.

Reflection Question FT.1: How has this exploration of faith-guided real estate investing influenced your understanding of stewardship?

Reflection Question FT.2: In what ways can your real estate investing serve God's purposes and reflect His character?

Journal Section FT.1: Describe your faith-guided real estate journey thus far. How have you grown, and where do you hope to go?

Journal Section FT.2: Reflect on the intersection of your faith and your investing. How can one inform and enrich the other moving forward?

Note:

_____

_____

These exercises, reflection questions, and journal prompts encourage a practical application of the principles discussed in Chapter 10 and the broader themes of the book. They invite you to contemplate your personal real estate journey from a faith-informed perspective and to plan for continued growth and learning.

References

Rich Dad Poor Dad Summary (Review & Book Notes).

https://bestwriting.com/book-notes/rich-dad-poor-dad